# "Norman Einstein"

# "NORMAN EINSTEIN"

## The Dis-Integration of Ken Wilber

### GEOFFREY D. FALK

Million Monkeys Press

Published by Million Monkeys Press
P.O. Box 68586
360A Bloor St. W.
Toronto, ON  M5S 3C9

Web: www.normaneinsteinbook.com

ISBN 978-0-9736203-4-4 (cloth)

Trademarks: "TM" and "Transcendental Meditation" are service marks registered in the U.S. Patent and Trademark Office, licensed to Maharishi Vedic Education Development Corporation. "Spiral Dynamics" is a registered trademark of the National Values Center, Inc.

**Library and Archives Canada Cataloguing in Publication**

Falk, Geoffrey D., 1966-
Norman Einstein : the dis-integration of Ken Wilber / Geoffrey D. Falk.

Includes bibliographical references and index.
Also available in electronic format.
ISBN 978-0-9736203-4-4 (bound).—ISBN 978-0-9736203-5-1 (pbk.)

1. Wilber, Ken.  I. Title.

BF109.W54F34 2009  191  C2009-900971-4

First edition.
10   9   8   7   6   5   4   3   2   1

# CONTENTS

Introduction ................................................................ vii

Chapter
I        Norman Einstein .............................................. 1
II       Wilberian Evolution ......................................... 5
III      Spiraling Psychology ........................................ 22
IV       Integral Meditation ......................................... 32
V        Kosmic Parapsychology ....................................... 49
VI       Wilberian Mathematics ....................................... 61
VII      Integral Politics ........................................... 63
VIII     Integral Censorship ......................................... 71
IX       Bald Narcissism ............................................. 90
X        The Strange Case of Ken Wilber .............................. 112
XI       Cargo Cult Philosophy ....................................... 133
XII      The Einstein of P.R. ........................................ 139

Appendix: Wilber and Bohm ........................................... 149
Bibliography ........................................................ 177
Index ............................................................... 201
About the Author .................................................... 205

# INTRODUCTION

When it comes to truth and justice there is no difference between the small and great problems. Whosoever fails to take small matters seriously in a spirit of truth cannot be trusted in greater affairs.

—Albert Einstein

[W]hen intellectual dishonesty (or gross incompetence) is discovered in one part—even a marginal part—of someone's writings, it is natural to want to examine more critically the rest of his or her work.

—Sokal and Bricmont, *Fashionable Nonsense*

Nobody in the game of football should be called a genius. A genius is somebody like Norman Einstein.

—former NFL quarterback Joe Theisman

THIS BOOK GREW OUT of a chapter and an appendix in the original online version of my second book, *Stripping the Gurus* (STG). Following the electronic publication of that, over the first half of 2006 I posted three additional appendices concerning the flaws in the ideas and character of Ken Wilber, with the material being presented there largely in the order in which it was written.

Here, the same information, with less commentary, has been regrouped by subject—although the "Bald Narcissism" chapter and the appendix on "Wilber and Bohm" remain largely as they were originally written.

Even with that new, non-chronological presentation, however, the chapters still provide an instructive example as to how even the most well-intentioned of spiritual communities will invariably degenerate into closed, unquestioning, cult-like environments.

Some of the information in several of the sections here was sparked by emails from Jim Andrews, whose research I have freely incorporated. Specifically, that refers to Wilber's pronouncements on animal cannibalism, the purported benefits and real dangers of meditation, the value of prayer, the "Maharishi Effect," and the supposed efficiency of yellow versus green value-memes.

February, 2009                                         Geoffrey D. Falk
Toronto, Ontario                                   www.geoffreyfalk.com

# "Norman Einstein"

CHAPTER I

# NORMAN EINSTEIN

To be thought enlightened, one must appear not only certain
that one is, but certain about most everything else, too
(Kramer and Alstad, 1993).

KEN WILBER IS THE "LONG-SOUGHT EINSTEIN of consciousness research," having been generously regarded as such since the late
1970s.

Ken Wilber is "a genius of our times."

Ken Wilber is "the foremost theoretician in transpersonal [and
integral] psychology."

Ken Wilber is "the world's most intriguing and foremost philosopher." To wit:

The twenty-first century literally has three choices: Aristotle,
Nietzsche, or Ken Wilber (Jack Crittenden, in [Wilber,
2000]).

Michael Murphy maintains that, along with Aurobindo's *Life
Divine*, Heidegger's *Being and Time*, and Whitehead's *Process and Reality*, Wilber's *Sex, Ecology, Spirituality* [SES] is

1

"one of the four great books of this [twentieth] century" (Integral, 2004).

Ken Wilber is "an American bodhisattva pandit."

Ken Wilber is "one of the most important pioneers in the field of consciousness in this century."

Ken Wilber is "a source of inspiration and insight to all of us."

Ken Wilber is "the most comprehensive philosophical thinker of our times."

Ken Wilber is "the most cogent and penetrating voice in the recent emergence of a uniquely American wisdom."

Ken Wilber is "the most influential integral thinker in the world today."

One need not search far at all to find glowing endorsements of the work which the esteemed Mr. Ken Wilber (or kw) has done over the past quarter of a century in consciousness studies. Indeed, the latter three of the above recommendations can be found, as of this writing, in the Ken Wilber section of his publisher's website (http://wilber.shambhala.com). The first two, further, come from one of *his own* (1991) books, via his late wife's diaries. Two others are only a click away from his home web page, nestled in an adoration-filled "update" on the value of his work, written by one of his long-time students (Reynolds, 2004).

Wilber began writing his first book at age twenty-three, having dropped out of postgraduate biochemistry studies in 1973 to pursue that activity. *The Spectrum of Consciousness* was rejected by at least twenty publishers over a three-year period (Schwartz, 1996) before finally being accepted by the Theosophical (Society's) Publishing House. Since then, Wilber has written over a dozen books. He has also acted (past tense) as an editor for both *ReVision* magazine and the New Science Library imprint of Shambhala, and had his *Collected Works* published by the same press.

Now in his early sixties, Wilber has founded and assumed the presidency of the Integral Institute (www.integralinstitute.org), or I-I, with its affiliated Integral University (IU) and Integral Naked forum. Guests of the latter have included spiritual luminaries such as Deepak Chopra, Carolyn Myss, and the Smashing Pumpkins' Billy Corgan.

Since 1995, Wilber's groundbreaking four-quadrant model of reality has been put to use by psychological, business and political leaders in America and beyond, under the acronym AQAL (All Quadrants, All Levels). Those four quadrants embrace the objective/exterior (e.g., in brain structure), subjective/interior (e.g., in psychological development and self-awareness), intersubjective (i.e., cultural) and interobjective (i.e., social) lives of the hierarchy of all relative wholes or "holons" in the cosmos. (The term "holon" was itself coined by Arthur Koestler.)

> In my opinion, this [four-quadrant] tool is one of the greatest inventions ever proposed for orienting human beings toward their own evolution (Van der Horst, 1997).

And yet—

> The model ... is largely descriptive. It organizes a great deal of phenomena, culled from investigations ranging over a wide range of disciplines in the natural and social sciences, and posits or implies that they are connected. But the model has very little to say about *how* they are [causally] connected. Wilber's silence on this question ... seriously undermines the model's usefulness for stimulating further research....
>
> In addition to not addressing the processes underlying the transitions from one level to another, Wilber's model also says little about the connections between phenomena in different quadrants.... How, for example, does a particular kind of consciousness become associated with a particular brain structure? How does a particular kind of social organization grow out of a particular kind of consciousness?
>
> Without answers to questions like these, Wilber's model can do no more than simply recognize that all these different phenomena exist. Nobody really questions that they do. What people do argue about is how they are related (Smith, 2001a; italics added).

As with Wilber's academic accolades, one need not search far at all to find indications of his high spiritual attainment. Indeed, already by the mid-'80s, Wilber (1991) could lay claim to "fifteen years of meditation, during which I had had several unmistakable 'kensho' [i.e., 'glimpse of enlightenment'] experiences, fully confirmed by my teachers."

Of course, nearly every "enlightened" individual in the spiritual marketplace has made fully comparable claims. That is, it is

rare to find a respected spiritual figure who has *not* received confirmation, from his own teachers or gurus, of his minor and major
enlightenment experiences. Thus, Wilber is part of a large class,
not a small one, in that regard. Such endorsements, indeed, mean
absolutely nothing, in terms of evaluating whether any given individual is enlightened or simply wildly deluded.

Nevertheless, Wilber's kensho experiences later blossomed
into the nondual "One Taste" state:

> I was conscious for eleven days and nights, even as the body
> and mind went through waking, dreaming, and sleeping: I
> was unmoved in the midst of changes; there was no I to be
> moved; there was only unwavering empty consciousness, the
> luminous mirror-mind, the witness that was one with every-
> thing witnessed. I simply reverted to what I am, and *it has
> been so, more or less, ever since* (Wilber, 2000a; italics added).

> Not even the Dalai Lama can sustain nondual awareness
> through deep sleep, Wilber informed me, as he can (Horgan,
> 2003a).

By any reasonable logic, that nondual realization would place
Wilber among the "truly great Zen masters" throughout history,
both in his own mind and objectively. That is so even should there
be states of realization beyond the One Taste experience, i.e., potentially making it not "the highest" possible understanding.

"All good things must come to an end," however—including,
apparently, the eternal, "always-already" One Taste realization:

> After attaining this [One Taste] ability in 1995, Wilber sus-
> tained it until about a year ago, when a nasty staph infection
> left him bedridden for six months. "I lost a great deal of ac-
> cess to it," he said, but "it's slowly coming back" (Horgan,
> 2003a).

CHAPTER II

# WILBERIAN EVOLUTION

From his footnotes and bibliographies alone, Wilber seems omniscient....

And as with meditation, clean living and exercise, one feels so much better after reading a little Wilber....

*A Brief History* ... is bound to seduce even the most casual reader into plunging into the intoxicating revelations of all the wise old trees to be found in the great magical Wilberness (Van der Horst, 1997).

NOTWITHSTANDING HIS REPUTATION as a brilliant academic, Wilber has grossly misrepresented basic, high-school-level concepts in evolutionary theory, in Chapter One of his (1996) *A Brief History of Everything*. Those misunderstandings have been analyzed devastatingly by David Lane (1996). The most damaging issues uncovered there relate to Wilber's expressed reluctance to believe that "half a wing" is better than none. In kw's own words:

Take the standard notion that wings simply evolved from forelegs. It takes perhaps a hundred mutations to produce a

5

functional wing from a leg—a half-wing is no good as a leg and no good as a wing—you can't run and you can't fly. It has no adaptive value whatsoever. In other words, with a half-wing you are dinner.

Richard Dawkins (1986), however, has elucidated the long-established facts of biology, regarding such "half-wings" and the like:

> There are animals alive today that beautifully illustrate every stage in the continuum. There are frogs that glide with big webs between their toes, tree-snakes with flattened bodies that catch the air, lizards with flaps along their bodies; and several different kinds of mammals that glide with membranes stretched between their limbs, showing us the kind of way bats must have got their start. Contrary to the creationist literature, not only are animals with "half a wing" common [i.e., they are not automatically "dinner"], so are animals with a quarter of a wing, three quarters of a wing, and so on.

Indeed, Darwin himself, in his (1962) *Origin of Species*—first published in 1859—recorded as much:

> Look at the family of squirrels; here we have the finest gradation from animals with their tails only slightly flattened, and from others ... with the posterior part of their bodies rather wide and with the skin on their flanks rather full, to the so-called flying squirrels.... We cannot doubt that each structure is of use [i.e., has adaptive value] to each kind of squirrel in its own country.

Nor does that exhaust the examples, even just from Darwin's own long-extant (1962) catalog:

> If about a dozen genera of birds were to become extinct or were unknown, who would have ventured to surmise that birds might have existed which used their wings solely as flappers, like the logger-headed duck (Micropterus of Eyton); as fins in the water and as front-legs on the land, like the penguin; as sails, like the ostrich; and functionally for no purpose, like the Apteryx? Yet the structure of each of these birds is good for it, under the conditions of life to which it is exposed....

Completely contrary to Wilber's confidently given presentation, then, half a wing certainly is better than none. Even penguins and ostriches know as much.

From being inexcusably wrong about that elementary idea, Wilber goes on to assert that "absolutely nobody" believes the "standard, glib, neo-Darwinian explanation" of chance mutation and natural selection anymore. In reprint editions (e.g., 2000c), that statement has been modified to read that "very few theorists" believe this anymore. Even being thus watered down, however, it still has no point of contact with reality:

> [Wilber's claim] is complete rubbish. Almost *everybody* who knows anything about biology does still believe this! (Carroll, 2003).

Dr. Lane—who has taught Darwinian evolution at a university level—then (1996) pertinently assessed Wilber's apparent comprehension of evolutionary biology:

> Wilber does not seem to understand that the processes of evolution are blind. He wants to have it "open-eyed" as if natural selection all of sudden wakes up when it hears that a "wing has been formed" (better start chugging) or that an "eye has been completed" (let's fine tune now). Natural selection does not "start" when the eye is formed; it works all along without any conscious intention whatsoever.
>
> Not to sound like a groggy professor, but if Wilber turned in [his written ideas] to me as a college student trying to explain the current view of evolutionary theory, I would give him an "F" and ask to see him in my office.... Wilber has misrepresented the fundamentals of natural selection. Moreover, his presentation of how evolution is viewed today is so skewed that Wilber has more in common with creationists than evolutionists, even though he is claiming to present the evolutionists' current view....
>
> What makes Wilber's remarks on evolution so egregious is ... that he so maligns and misrepresents the current state of evolutionary biology, suggesting that he is somehow on top of what is currently going on in the field.
>
> And Wilber does it by exaggeration, by false statements, and by rhetoric license.

And how have Wilber and his entourage reacted to such eminently valid points? As Jack Crittenden—who used to co-edit the *ReVision* journal with Wilber—put it (in Integral, 2004):

> Wilber has not been believably criticized for misunderstanding or misrepresenting any of the fields of knowledge that he includes [in his four-quadrant "Theory of Everything"].

That statement, of course, has been false since at least 1996, given Lane's wonderful work and the fact that Wilber's "Theory of Everything" most certainly includes basic evolution.

In May of 2005, Wilber offered a rather hasty defense of his documented misrepresentations and arguable misunderstandings of high-school-level evolution theory. From the Integral Naked web forum, via the Vomiting Confetti blog:

> Folks, give me a break on this one. I have a Master's degree in biochemistry, and a Ph.D. minus thesis in biochemistry and biophysics, with specialization in the mechanism of the visual process. I did my thesis on the photoisomerization of rhodopsin in bovine rod outer segments. I know evolutionary theory inside out, including the works of Dawkins et al.... Instead of a religious preacher like Dawkins, start with something like Michael Behe's *Darwin's Black Box: The Biochemical Challenge to Evolution*. And then guess what? Neo-Darwinian theory can't explain shit. Deal with it....
>
> The problem is that creation scientists—who are almost entirely Christians—after having convincingly demonstrated that neo-Darwinian theory has loopholes large enough to drive several Hummers through—then try to prove that Jehovah is in one of the Hummers....
>
> But all that this ["failure" of neo-Darwinian theory] really proves, in my opinion, is that there is an Eros to the Kosmos, an Eros that scientific evolutionary theory as it is simply cannot explain. But overall integral theory doesn't hang on that particular issue. If physicalistic, materialistic, reductionistic forces turn out to give an adequate explanation to the extraordinary diversity of evolutionary unfolding, then fine, that is what we will include in integral theory. And if not, not. But so far, the "nots" have it by a staggeringly huge margin, and scientists when they are not bragging to the world, whisper this to themselves every single day of their lives.

None of the above, however, alters the fact that Wilber has completely misrepresented the truth that half-wings *do* exist, and have been documented as existing since Darwin's own *Origin of Species*. That has nothing to do with any (excusable) popularizing of Wilber's theories on his own part. Rather, it is simply a gross and brutally dishonest misrepresentation of basic *facts* by him, to suit his own "integral" purposes. That is true independent of whether or not kw understands how evolution works.

Since when, though, is one allowed to misrepresent such elementary facts as the above, even in popularizing one's ideas? What respected academic has ever done that? Simplifying the Ph.D.-level complexities is one thing; misrepresenting high-school-level ideas (with no caveats whatsoever to that effect in the text) is another issue entirely.

Plus, the points on which kw has messed up are literally taught in high school. For whom was he then "dumbing down" those ideas, if even high-school students can understand them in their real nature?

And as to Michael Behe, minimal research discloses:

Intelligent Design has been a wholesale failure, as both science and strategy. None of its scientific claims, especially the work of the main theorists William Dembski and Michael Behe, have stood up under scientific scrutiny. None of their claims is [sic] published in scientific journals. Numerous books and articles refute their positions in great detail. Not only have their arguments been shown to be flawed, but in several instances, the factual claims on which they rest have been proven false (Stenger, 2004).

Richard Dawkins (2008) further notes:

Behe simply proclaims the bacterial flagellar motor to be irreducibly complex. Since he offers no argument in favor of his assertion, we may begin by suspecting a failure of his imagination. He further alleges that specialist biological literature has ignored the problem. The falsehood of this allegation was massively and (to Behe) embarrassingly documented in the court of Judge John E. Jones in Pennsylvania in 2005, where Behe was testifying as an expert witness on behalf of a group of creationists who had tried to impose "intelligent design" creationism on the science curriculum of a local public school—a move of "breathtaking inanity," to quote Judge Jones....

If you take Behe seriously, please further read Pigliucci's (2001) critique of Intelligent Design theory and Neocreationism. From which:

> To be sure, there are several cases in which biologists do not know enough about the fundamental constituents of the cell to be able to hypothesize or demonstrate their gradual evolution. But this is rather an argument from ignorance, not positive evidence of irreducible complexity. William Paley advanced exactly the same argument to claim that it is impossible to explain the appearance of the eye by natural means. Yet, today biologists know of several examples of intermediate forms of the eye, and there is evidence that this structure evolved several times independently during the history of life on Earth.

Nice example; and ironic, too, given Wilber's own research with cows' *eyes,* and his consistent use of the same type of sophomoric "arguments from ignorance" to find room for his own transpersonal notions and willing acceptance of parapsychological claims, within real science.

Further,

> Although the [Intelligent Design] movement is loosely allied with, and heavily funded by, various conservative Christian groups—and although ID plainly maintains that life was created—it is generally silent about the identity of the creator (Orr, 2005).

Not exactly *Jehovah* in a Hummer, then, is it?

And Wilber's claim that integral theorizers will abide by physical science if it can "explain everything" is extremely disingenuous: He will do no such thing, ever. For, his "theories" have been shot through with *koshas* (i.e., astral and causal bodies), auras, subtle energies, chakras and the like from the start. That is, he has made his living, from the beginning, theorizing on the basis of completely unvetted and unsound data, and continues to do so to the present day.

So what we have here from Wilber are no documented facts, no relevant details, just his "Einsteinian" authority, his rampant hyperbole, and a laughable appeal to other discredited "thinkers" to back up his own claims to expertise.

If kw wants to make wild claims about the "failures" of Darwinian evolution in courtroom contexts and otherwise, he needs to do *way* more than simply throw out a smoke-screen of unsubstantiated claims (plus one book title).

And why did it take him nearly a *decade* to give any response at all to what is effectively just more of David Lane's critique of his misunderstandings of basic evolution, from 1996? Did he think that *devastating* critique was just going to go away?

In his most-recent (2006e) text, *Integral Spirituality*—"possibly the most important spiritual book in postmodern times," according to the blurbing roshi Dennis Genpo Merzel—Wilber again made the following claim:

> Proponents of ID have one truth on their side: scientific materialism cannot explain all of evolution (it can explain pretty much everything except major holistic transformational leaps). With that, I quite agree.

Since kw gave no examples there of such "major holistic transformational leaps," however, one could reasonably have assumed that he was referring to the evolutionary development of wings and eyes, etc.—neither of which provide any challenge at all to neo-Darwinian evolution.

None of this, again, has anything to do with simple popularizations of integral theories, were those to be done with proper forthrightness. It is rather just an appeal to basic intellectual honesty and minimal academic competence. Other fields of knowledge have that. That is what makes them worth spending time understanding.

So what does real science, then, have to say about Behe and his ilk?

> [I]n 2002, the American Association for the Advancement of Science (AAAS) passed a resolution declaring "intelligent design" to be a "philosophical or theological concept," not a statement obtained through the examination of hard evidence, and that it should not be taught in science classes. That's 120,000 men and women of science, honored and respected internationally, who have the experience, the knowl-

edge, and the training to be able to understand and authoritatively declare on such matters (Randi, 2005).

Which "real scientists" then, are the ones whom Wilber thinks are siding with him? Perhaps the following, from the www.skepticalinvestigations.org website:

In a new paper Ted Dace contends that the dispute between the rival views of evolution is between two failed theories. The mechanistic ideology of neo-Darwinism weakens the case for evolution and leaves the field clear for creationism. Sheldrake and Elsasser have found a basis for the inheritance of adaptations making this endless clash of ideologies redundant.

As an exercise for anyone with even a high-school knowledge of how evolution works: Poke SUV-sized holes in the following, embarrassingly off-the-mark objections to neo-Darwinian evolution, from the same paper:

The Hyacinth macaw can crack a nut with its beak that you or I would need a sledgehammer to open. Is all that colossal strength nothing more than a side-effect of a chance mutation in the macaw's genetic toolkit? How many millions of such coding mistakes had to come and go before the right one announced itself, and at last the bird got its meal?

So stupendously unlikely is the *perfect mutation at the perfect time* that calculating the odds against it taking place even once exceeds our imaginative capacity. It is, in fact, a miracle (Dace, 2005; italics added).

Note again that Wilber has claimed that he was deliberately oversimplifying his comparable presentation of the mechanism of evolution—and thus apparently *intentionally deceiving* his readers —in a book intended for the general public. Yet, his cohorts in "integral skepticism" quite clearly believe exactly what he claims to have purposely wrongly presented. (Larry Dossey and Gary Schwartz are both "Associates and Advisors" of the Skeptical Investigations site. They are also founding members of Wilber's Integral Institute.)

Whether or not any of the other avant-garde claims made in Dace's paper are valid, when perfect nonsense (or deliberate deceptions, take your pick) like the above regarding "perfect mutations" and probabilities is presented as if it were insightful wisdom, one is being generous in even reading further.

More recently, Wilber (2007) has touted the immune system as something which supposedly cannot be accounted for on the basis of neo-Darwinian evolution:

> [T]he complex forms of evolution that we see—such as the immune system—are not the products of mere chance mutation and natural selection....

Interestingly, Richard Dawkins makes the following related point, in his (2008) *The God Delusion:*

> Another of Behe's favorite alleged examples of "irreducible complexity" is the immune system. Let Judge Jones himself take up the story:
>
> > In fact, on cross-examination, Professor Behe was questioned concerning his 1996 claim that science would never find an evolutionary explanation for the immune system. He was presented with fifty-eight peer-reviewed publications, nine books, and several immunology textbook chapters about the evolution of the immune system; however, he simply insisted that this was still not sufficient evidence of evolution, and that it was not "good enough."
>
> Behe, under cross-examination by Eric Rothschild, chief counsel for the plaintiffs, was forced to admit that he hadn't read most of those fifty-eight peer-reviewed papers.... After listening to Behe, Rothschild eloquently summed up what every honest person in that courtroom must have felt:
>
> > Thankfully, there are scientists who do search for answers to the question of the origin of the immune system.... It's our defense against debilitating and fatal diseases. The scientists who wrote those books and articles toil in obscurity, without book royalties or speaking engagements. Their efforts help us combat and cure serious medical conditions. By contrast, Professor Behe and the entire intelligent design movement [like Wilber with his Eros-fixation] are doing nothing to advance scientific or

medical knowledge and are telling future genera-
tions of scientists, don't bother.

In connection with Wilber's recent emphasis on the immune
system as ostensibly showing the action of Eros, he has also been
unconvincingly insisting that his original claims about half-wings
offering no evolutionary advantage were never meant to be taken
seriously, i.e., that they were intended just as metaphors. It is not
difficult to guess as to why he has changed his emphasis, and attempted to rewrite his own history.

First, note that Behe's *Darwin's Black Box* was first published
(and largely refuted) in 1996, being reviewed in *Nature* in September of that year. Thus, kw could not, in principle have read it and
referenced its ideas while writing *A Brief History of Everything,*
which was published before the end of the same year. (In the publishing industry, there is typically at least a nine-month delay between the finishing of a manuscript and its official publication
date.)

Wilber's ABHOE mentions the immune system only once ...
and that one mention is given, ironically, in a strictly metaphorical
context.

Thus, a very reasonable inference would be that kw has been
so comfortable in recently back-pedaling about his "half-wing"
claims only because he now has a "better" example, from Behe,
which he *hadn't even known about back in 1996,* when he was writing ABHOE. So, he can dismiss his own earlier, false claims about
the supposed uselessness of half-wings as being *intended* only as
metaphors, and can further belittle anyone who took them seriously as having supposedly missed his point:

> I am fully aware that selection carries forth each previous se-
> lection (which still has problems in itself ... why would a half
> wing make running easier???), but even if you give that to
> the evolutionists (which I am willing to do), it still has this
> gaping hole in it.... [W]ings or eyes ... are metaphors and ex-
> amples for this extraordinary capacity of creative emergence
> that is intrinsic to the universe (exactly as Whitehead ex-
> plained it). So, no, I don't take this criticism of my work seri-
> ously, although it is a good example of flatland thinking
> (Wilber, 2007).

Interestingly, Kenneth Dial has recently showed (see Haugland, 2004) that having half a wing actually *does* make running easier for partridge chicks, but that is just lucky happenstance in this context. What is more relevant is that there is no reason why both of those skills (i.e., flying and running) should be simultaneously maximized in any species, much less that any single attribute/mutation should increase the ability to do both of them. Obviously, all that is needed for a mutation to be retained by the species is for the *net* effect of it to yield a slight survival advantage.

> Organisms don't evolve toward every imaginable advantage. If they did, every creature would be faster than a speeding bullet, more powerful than a locomotive, and able to leap tall buildings in a single bound. An organism that devotes some of its matter and energy to one organ must take it away from another. It must have thinner bones or less muscle or fewer eggs. Organs evolve only when their benefits outweigh their costs (Pinker, 1999).

In his (2005a) interview with Alan Wallace on Integral Naked, Wilber further asserted:

> The closure principle doesn't explain why dirt gets up and starts writing poetry. It's incomprehensible to me that somebody can actually look at you with a straight face and say something like that. Nonetheless, there are a lot of them out there at Jane Loevinger's stage five and they all seem to believe it.

Wilber's emphasis on poetry there is likely just a convenient "leader" into the transpersonal realms; what he is really trying to sneak in is that "dirt can't get up and consciously experience the astral or causal realms, or rest in the Witness" without Eros to animate it. That is, even if dirt could get up and write poetry, by whatever algorithmically expressible laws, it could never evolve into astral, causal and transcendent stages or levels of consciousness. So, Wilber's frequent mention of poetry is just the "thin edge of the wedge" which he wants to use to sneak Eros into the Kosmos: if he can get you to (wrongly) grant him that poetry is an "emergent" phenomenon, he will be very quick to parlay that all the way up the Great Chain of Being.

And yet, contrary to the idea that there is some esoteric force involved in the creation of art, the prolific inventor and futurist

Ray Kurzweil has built a "Cybernetic Poet" program, which "analyzes word sequences from patterns of poems it has 'read' using markov models (a mathematical cousin of neural nets [and also widely used in automatic speech-recognition programs])." It then creates new poetry based on those patterns ... just as other programs have created music in particular styles:

> In 1997, Steve Larson, a University of Oregon music professor, arranged a musical variation of the Turing Test by having an audience attempt to determine which of three pieces of music had been written by a computer and which one of the three had been written two centuries ago by a human named Johann Sebastian Bach.... [T]he audience selected the piece written by a computer program named EMI (Experiments in Musical Intelligence) to be the authentic Bach composition (Kurzweil, 2000).

Wilber has, by now (2007), reduced his notion of Eros to potentially being "[not] a metaphysical force, just an intrinsic force of self-organization"—yet still apparently *in addition to* the self-organization reasonably modeled by legitimate scientists like Stuart Kauffman. That is again being done on the pretense that more self-organization is needed in the Kosmos, to explain poetry and intelligence, etc., than materialistic science can provide.

Yet, as Steven Pinker (in Schneider, 2007; italics added) has noted:

> Intelligence is a gadget that is selected when its benefits (in particular, outsmarting the defenses of other plants and animals) outweigh the costs (a big, injury-prone, birth-complicating, metabolically expensive organ bobbling on top of your neck). And that probably happens only for certain kinds of organisms in certain ecologically circumstances. *It isn't a general goal of evolution, or else we'd see humanlike intelligence repeatedly evolving.* Since elephants and humans have not been primary ecological competitors for most of the evolutionary history of the elephant, it's unlikely that they've been waiting for humans to get out of the way before getting smarter. It's more likely that they are at an adaptive plateau in which still-better brains aren't worth the cost.

If Eros was really behind it all, pushing intelligence to emerge in all species, why wouldn't elephants have evolved the same (or greater) cognitive capacities as humans have? Why would It have pushed our particular species harder, to develop a more complex (but smaller) brain? If the Goal of the Kosmos was to express Divine Intelligence, why wouldn't elephants have evolved to be literal Ganeshes? *What was stopping them,* particularly since "Every organism alive today has had the same amount of time to evolve since the origin of life"?

> In many lineages, of course, animals have become more complex. Life began simple, so the complexity of the *most* complex creature alive on earth at any time has to increase over the eons. But in many lineages they have not. The organisms reach an optimum and stay put, often for hundreds of millions of years. And those that do become more complex don't always become smarter.... Evolution is about ends, not means; becoming smart [via the interconnections and algorithms of a complex network of neurons, called a brain] is just one option (Pinker, 1999).

Wilber (in Phipps, 2007) has also tried to relate evolution to the idea that higher stages of development necessarily "transcend and include" their precursors:

> Evolution goes beyond what went before, but because it must embrace what went before, then its very nature is to transcend and include [and thus to become more complex], and thus it has an inherent directionality, a secret impulse [of progress] toward increasing depth, increasing intrinsic value, increasing consciousness.

But, as Jeff Meyerhoff has noted, in his (2006d) "Dismissal Vs. Debate":

> For Wilber, progress ... is determined by increased complexity defined as greater transcendence and inclusion.
>
> Many biological organisms find their adaptive success [i.e., their "survivability"] in becoming simpler after a more complex beginning [and thus not "including" all that went before them in their own evolution]....
>
> So Wilber cannot use survivability as his criterion of progress because then he will have no justification for structuring his entire integral hierarchy around increased complexity. His whole model of universal movement from the Big

Bang to the present moment as one of directed evolution towards increased complexity is seriously skewed towards a
relatively minor natural phenomenon....

In late June of 2006, Jim Chamberlain posted his own comments on Wilber's misrepresentations of biological evolution, on
Frank Visser's Integral World (www.integralworld.net) website:

> Wilber adds the word "clearly" to the last sentence [of a
> quote from Ernst Mayr's book *What Evolution Is,* regarding
> the "progressive" nature of evolution] and he says it with
> great emphasis, but it does not appear in the book.

Wilber responded with a (2006d; italics added) blog entry, after Chamberlain's above claim had been shown to be incorrect:

> [S]cholars in particular should accept no statements on the
> Visser site about what my position is....
> I am saying that categorically the posts at that site are
> not to be trusted or accepted in any academic discourse as
> representing my actual views. *They lie over there,* so be care-
> ful. I'm sorry, but the site is so sleazy, one critic [actually,
> one of kw's integral friends] called it the equivalent of the
> Penthouse Letters to the editor....
> I'm warning scholars to stay away from this when it
> comes to academic discussions of my work.

From Chamberlain's subsequent apology for his error:

> Mayr said "clearly" and Wilber quoted him accurately and I
> made a stupid mistake by stating otherwise. For that I
> apologize to Ken.

Not to at all excuse Chamberlain's rather mind-boggling error,
but: even the formal "editorial integrity" with which Wilber's own
work has been evaluated by his publisher/friend Samuel Bercholz
at Shambhala, for one, didn't stop his presentation of evolutionary
biology in *A Brief History of Everything* from being, in Robert Carroll's (2003) words, "a few paragraphs of half-truths and lies." Nor
did it stop kw from ridiculously misrepresenting David Bohm's
ideas on quantum physics, in his embarrassingly amateurish *The
Holographic Paradigm and Other Paradoxes.* Nor did it constrain

his wildly hyperbolic, unprovoked ranting against Bohm in *The Eye of Spirit,* as disclosed in this book's appendix.

If what Chamberlain has done is to "lie" rather than just make a "stupid mistake," then Wilber is subject to exactly the same charge, many times over, for his numerous provable fabrications of purported "facts." That is, as we shall see repeatedly, he himself could hardly be more guilty than he already is of the very same misrepresentations that he finds in Chamberlain's piece.

Chamberlain, though, at least had the decency to apologize for his inexcusable "stupid mistake." Where is the same integrity in kw when *he* gets caught provably fabricating information in an attempt to either support his own "theories" or discredit the work of his "competitors"?

Interestingly, in addition to his gross misrepresentations of high-school-level evolutionary theory, Wilber has equally falsely presented the facts of animal warfare and cannibalism.

First, in his (1983a) *Up from Eden,* kw had this to say regarding the supposed psychological and spiritual causes underlying war and the "substitute sacrifice" of human murder:

> [U]nder the desire to kill lies the extroverted death impact, and under death impact lies the pull of transcendence. Murder, that is, is a form of substitute sacrifice or substitute transcendence. Homicide is the new form of the Atman project. The deepest wish of all is to sacrifice one's self—"kill" it —so as to find true transcendence and Atman; but, failing that, one arranges the *substitute* sacrifice of actually killing somebody else, thus acting on, and appeasing, the terrifying confrontation with death and Thanatos....
>
> I am not denying the existence of simple, instinctive, biological aggression, in mammals or in humans. The coyote does aggress—but not out of hatred. As Ashley Montagu put it, the coyote doesn't kill the rabbit because it hates the rabbit but because it loves the rabbit the way I love ice cream. **Man—and only man**—regularly kills out of *hatred,* and for that we will have to look elsewhere than the genes....
>
> I am suggesting that, in the cognitive elaboration between simple biological aggression and wanton human murder, death and death terror become all-significantly interwoven into the final motivation....

> Aggression and mass homicide, in the form of war, generally began ... with the [agrarian] mythic-membership structure.

And yet, from the December, 1995, *National Geographic* article by Peter Miller on "Jane Goodall," concerning Goodall's decades-long field studies of chimps in Tanzania:

> Frequently tender and compassionate, humanity's closest living relatives are also capable of scheming, deceiving, **and waging war**....
>
> By the end of the conflict, the Kahama community— seven males and three adult females and their young—had been annihilated. Researchers witnessed five of the attacks, in which the Kasakela chimps tore at their victims' flesh with their teeth as if they were common prey.

Goodall's best guess as to the origins of that extermination? That the territorial Kasakela males were taking back land which they had previously occupied. That was purely a guess on her part, though, to try and make sense of the chimps' actions.

The warring of those chimps was actually disclosed by Goodall as early as a May, 1979, *National Geographic* article—several years before Wilber's copyrighting of *Up from Eden.*

So, quite obviously, Wilber has again inexcusably gotten his *basic* facts wrong, there. That is even aside from his more-recent (1996) admission that 58% of foraging (i.e., pre-agrarian, pre-mythic-membership) cultures engaged in "frequent or intermittent warfare." Yet amazingly, as recently as 1996, in the same *A Brief History of Everything,* he was still insisting that apes do not make war. (Chimps are apes of equatorial Africa.)

If one sticks to the properly vetted data, it is clear that chimps (and dolphins too, apparently) are just as capable of extended warring as are human beings, for what look to be quite comparable reasons and emotions.

One assumes, though, that any "cognizance of their own mortality," and consequent transpersonally hypothesized "substitute sacrifice" on the part of the chimps and dolphins, wouldn't really enter into it!

From kw's (2003c) *Kosmic Consciousness,* CD 5 Track 3, beginning at 4:39, we further learn:

[T]estosterone is one component of a dickhead, kick-ass attitude that we all know and love as the human male. And it's also human males, rats, and weasels are the only three animals that kill their own kind. So I think that sort of says something as well.

However, we already knew, from our respective days in high-school biology, that the female praying mantis cannibalizes the male after sex. Indeed, even as early as 1978, *Time* magazine published an article, "Animals That Kill Their Young." The piece begins:

In his classic work *On Aggression,* Nobel Laureate Konrad Lorenz argued that man is the only species that regularly kills its own kind. This concept, which contrasted the order and restraint in the animal world with the chaotic aggressiveness of man, reflected the mood of the time: the shadow-of-the-Bomb pessimism of the '50s and early '60s. But Lorenz was wrong; since 1963, when his book was published, naturalists have identified dozens of species that kill their own, including lions, hippos, bears, wolves, hyenas, herring gulls and more than fifteen types of primates other than man.

Lorenz's *On Aggression* is item #267 in the bibliography for Wilber's (1983a) *Up from Eden*—being a woefully outdated source of information even at that point. Note, though, that even when kw has updated his "expert" knowledge (as of 2003), he is still more than *twenty-five years* behind anything resembling a competent, current understanding of the field.

# CHAPTER III

# SPIRALING
# PSYCHOLOGY

WILBER WAS FOR MANY YEARS FETED as the "foremost theoretician in transpersonal psychology," until his voluntary abandoning of that field to found his own, more-inclusive "integral psychology." Thus, one might reasonably hope that, whatever shortcomings exist in his knowledge of other fields, his understanding and presentation of core ideas in psychology would stand up to thorough questioning.

However, as early as 1993, kw's understanding of Carl Jung's ideas regarding archetypes was seriously questioned by the Jungian psychologist V. Walter Odajnyk, in Appendix A of his *Gathering the Light*. Indeed, Odajnyk there explicitly regarded Wilber as having an "erroneous view" of Jung's position:

> Wilber's criticism of Jung's notion of archetypes is misinformed. Contrary to what Wilber states, Jung *does* refer to the archetypes as "the patterns upon which all other manifestations are based"....
>
> [Further,] contrary to what Wilber claims, Jung does not locate the archetypes only at the beginning of the evolution-

22

ary spectrum—they are present both at the beginning and at the end....

The spirit Mercurius is the archetype that expresses the notion, stated much too generally by Wilber, that "the ascent of consciousness was drawn *toward* the archetypes *by* the archetypes themselves." Far from being a criticism of Jung, this was Jung's discovery and not Wilber's....

[Likewise,] it is Jung and not Wilber who first proposed clear distinctions among "collective prepersonal, collective personal, and collective transpersonal" elements of the psyche [cf. Wilber's celebrated "pre/trans fallacy" insights where, because both pre-rational and transrational claims are "non-rational," they are often wrongly equated].

Note further that Odajnyk's critique was given well prior to Crittenden's assertion—first made in 1998, and reprinted by Wilber's own Integral Institute in 2004—that no "believable criticisms" have ever been made of kw's representations of others' work. Further, Odajnyk's book was put into print by Wilber's own long-time publisher, Shambhala. Thus, kw could not reasonably have been unaware of its existence.

Odajnyk's comments on Wilber's early work, too, are worth noting:

When it comes to psychological development, we know that it is possible to point out a person, or a culture, with highly evolved intelligence and consciousness while his, or its, instinctive, emotional, and ethical development lags far behind .... In other words, it is possible to have a higher consciousness that is "transcendent, transpersonal, and transtemporal" and a personal unconscious that is "instinctive, impulsive, libidinous, id-ish, animal, ape-like." I know that for Wilber [in his early work, pre-1981] this is not possible by definition, but definition is theory.

Wilber's more recent (see 2000e) psychological model includes more than a dozen "streams" of development, or quasi-independent "lines"—of cognition, needs, sexuality, motivation, self-identity, etc. Those lines were first introduced by kw (1998) in his "Wilber-3" phase, beginning in the early '80s. And such epicyclic streams/lines do indeed now allow for individuals to be simultaneously at, for example, a high level of cognitive or of psychic/spiritual development, but a low moral stage.

In his discussions of psychological stage-growth, Wilber has referenced Jean Piaget's work since his (kw's) early-'80s books *The Atman Project* and *Up from Eden.* Chapter 11 of his *A Brief History of Everything* further has this to say regarding Piaget's concrete operational and formal operational stages:

> Around the age of 11–15 years in our culture, the capacity for formal operational awareness emerges.... Where concrete operational awareness ["conop," from around age seven] can operate on the concrete world, formal operational awareness can operate on thought itself. It's not just thinking about the world, it's thinking about thinking....
>
> There's also a classical [*sic*] experiment that Piaget used to spot this extremely important emergence or paradigm shift or worldview shift. In simplified versions: the person is given three glasses of clear liquid and told that they can be mixed in a way that will produce a yellow color. The person is then asked to produce the yellow color.
>
> Concrete operational children will simply start mixing the liquids together haphazardly. They will keep doing this until they stumble on the right combination or give up. In other words, as the name implies, they perform *concrete operations*—they have to actually do it in a concrete way.
>
> Formal operational adolescents will first form a general picture of the fact that you have to try glass A with glass B, then A with C, then B with C, and so on. If you ask them about it, they will say something like, "Well, I need to try all the various combinations one at a time." In other words, they have a formal operation in their mind, a scheme that lets them know that you have to try *all the possible* combinations.

Piaget (2000), in his own books, actually described using *five* jars of clear liquid—labeled "A" through "E"—not three. Note, though, that kw did explicitly state that he was presenting a "simplified" version of the experiment—exactly what he failed to state with regard to his misrepresentations of basic evolution *in the same book.* If one takes that as being significant, it only makes it more likely that, in spite of his subsequent claims to the contrary, his misrepresentations of Darwinian evolution came precisely from failing to understand it even at a high-school level. That is, the pattern would make him more honest, but less competent.

In any case, M.I.T.'s Seymour Papert (1993), inventor of the LOGO (Turtle) programming language and math-learning environment, had this to say about the individual's evolution from the conop to the formop stage:

> What is the nature of the difference between the so-called "concrete" operations involved in conservation [e.g., where the results of counting do not depend on the order in which the relevant objects are counted, or where the volume of a liquid remains the same whether it is in a tall or a short glass] and the so-called "formal" operations involved in the combinatorial task? The names given them by Piaget and the empirical data suggest a deep and essential difference.
>
> [But from] a computational point of view, the most salient ingredients of the combinatorial task are related to the idea of procedure—systematicity and debugging. A successful solution consists of following some such procedure as:
>
> - Separate the beads into colors
> - Choose a color A as color 1
> - Form all the pairs that can be formed with color 1
> - Choose color 2
> - Form all the pairs that can be formed with color 2
> - Do this for each color
> - Go back and remove the duplicates
>
> So what is really involved is writing and executing a program including the all-important debugging step. This observation suggests a reason for the fact that children acquire this ability so late: Contemporary culture provides relatively little opportunity for *bricolage* [i.e., do-it-yourself "experimentation"] with the elements of systematic procedures of this type....
>
> [Endnote: Of course our culture provides everyone with plenty of occasions to *practice* particular systematic procedures. Its poverty is in materials for *thinking about* and *talking about* procedures....]
>
> I see no reason to doubt that this difference could account for a gap of five years or more between the ages at which conservation of number and combinatorial abilities are acquired....

It may well be universally true of precomputer societies that *numerical* knowledge would be more richly represented than *programming* knowledge. It is not hard to invent plausible explanations of such a cognitive-social universal. But things may be different in the computer-rich cultures of the future. If computers and programming become a part of the daily life of children, the conservation-combinatorial gap will surely close and **could conceivably be reversed: Children may learn to be systematic** [a purportedly distinguishing characteristic of formop, and one standard experimental "proof" that a child is at that stage of development] **before they learn to be quantitative** [in conop]!

Papert (1993) worked with Piaget himself for five years in Switzerland, from 1959 to 1964; he knows what he is talking about on this subject.

Even worse for Wilber's reputation, his oft-given claim of a consensus in the developmental-psychology field with regard to Piaget's studies is demonstrably false:

Piaget's theory of cognitive development is central to Wilber's description of the individual's interior development. Yet in my chapter on individual development [in *Bald Ambition*] I cite five professors of psychology [who seriously question the sturdiness of Piaget's ideas, even to the point of narrating a "collapse of Piagetian theory"], all with concentrations in developmental psychology....

Wilber, writing a few years after these negative assessments, writes that "as for the cognitive line itself, Piaget's work is still very impressive; moreover, after almost three decades of intense cross-cultural research, the evidence is virtually unanimous: Piaget's stages up to formal operational are universal and cross-cultural" (Meyerhoff, 2006b).

In Wilber's *A Brief History of Everything*, he further had this to say regarding the cognitive spectrum:

Take, for example, the work of Howard Gardner on multiple intelligences—the idea that development involves not one capacity but many relatively independent capacities (from musical to artistic to mathematical to athletic, and so on), **which I think is quite right**. We can plot the depth of those developmental capacities as well. They will fall within the same basic levels of consciousness development, but they are nonetheless relatively separate talents that unfold with their own logics, as it were. None of that is denied; in fact, I very much support those approaches. In my view, there are numerous different developmental lines or streams (e.g., cognitive, moral, aesthetic, interpersonal, needs, etc.) that move relatively independently through the basic levels or waves (body to mind to soul to spirit), giving us a very rich, multidimensional tapestry of waves and streams of consciousness unfolding.

However, Linda Gottfredson (1998) has noted, of the same alleged "multiple intelligences":

Several decades of factor-analytic research on mental tests have confirmed a hierarchical model of mental abilities. The evidence ... puts g [i.e., "general intelligence"] at the apex in this model, with more specific aptitudes arrayed at successively lower levels: the so-called group factors, such as verbal ability, mathematical reasoning, spatial visualization and memory, are just below g, and below these are skills that are more dependent on knowledge or experience, such as the principles and practices of a particular job or profession.

Some researchers use the term "multiple intelligences" to label these sets of narrow capabilities and achievements. Psychologist Howard Gardner of Harvard University, for example, has postulated that eight relatively autonomous "intelligences" are exhibited in different domains of achievement. He does not dispute the existence of g but treats it as a specific factor relevant chiefly to academic achievement and to situations that resemble those of school. Gardner does not believe that tests can fruitfully measure his proposed intelligences; without tests, no one can at present determine whether the intelligences are indeed independent of g (or each other). Furthermore, it is not clear to what extent Gardner's intelligences tap personality traits or motor skills rather than mental aptitudes.

Other forms of intelligence have been proposed; among them, emotional intelligence and practical intelligence are perhaps the best known. They are probably amalgams either of intellect and personality or of intellect and informal experience in specific job or life settings, respectively. Practical intelligence like "street smarts," for example, seems to con-

sist of the localized knowledge and know-how developed with
untutored experience in particular everyday settings and activities—the so-called school of hard knocks. In contrast,
general intelligence is not a form of achievement, whether local or renowned. Instead the $g$ factor regulates the rate of
learning: it greatly affects the rate of return in knowledge to
instruction and experience but cannot substitute for either.

Steven Pinker (in Schneider, 2007) likewise concluded:

I'm sympathetic to modular theories of the generic human
mind like Howard Gardner's, but they have nothing to do
with individual differences in intelligence. For one thing, the
inclusion of "musical" and "bodily and kinesthetic" intelligence is mainly a tactic to morally elevate those traits by re-
branding them as forms of "intelligence." But a great athlete
or drummer is not necessarily "intelligent" in the sense that
people ordinarily mean by the term.

In more recent years, beginning with his (2001) novel *Boomeritis,* Wilber has focused on Spiral Dynamics® (SD), based on the
work of Clare Graves, as a convenient way of categorizing stages of
human psychological development. (It is not necessary, for the present purposes, to understand exactly what Spiral Dynamics is, in
all of its details. The interested reader may wish to consult Don
Beck and Christopher Cowan's [2005] *Spiral Dynamics: Mastering
Values, Leadership and Change.*)

Interestingly, while Beck was a founding member of the Integral Institute, his former partner Cowan (www.spiraldynamics
.org) has actually commented very unfavorably on Wilber's comprehension of SD:

[Wilber's presentations of Spiral Dynamics] twist the theory
and contain glib over-simplifications and biases ... which reflect neither the nuances nor the intent of this theory. There
is frequent confusion of values with Value Systems. He also
seems to have trouble differentiating the levels of psychological existence from personality traits ... and grossly misunder-
stands and overplays the "tier" notion....

Much of the material demonstrates a very limited grasp
of the underlying theory ... he's wrong far more often than
there's any excuse for. Thus, the supposed SD foundation on

which he builds so many arguments is fundamentally, fatally flawed....

[Wilber] is putting out impressive-sounding junk and nonsense that must be undone if the integrity of the model is to be protected. There's no excuse for it (Cowan, 2005).

Because Wilber tries to apply but doesn't actually understand Gravesian theory, he confuses the levels/colors like a novice. He doesn't know green from orange or yellow. Thus, the elaborate arguments he lays out are constructed on quicksand.... And because he sounds authoritative, newcomers to SD will believe they're getting a valid overview of Graves/SD from *Boomeritis* (Cowan, 2002).

In one of his attempted practical applications of Spiral Dynamics, on page 396 of *Boomeritis,* Wilber has "Charles Morin" assert the following:

Studies [not cited by kw] show that yellow [value-meme, level seven] is approximately **ten times more efficient than green** [level six]....

[I]f 10% of the population is at yellow, it will very likely be at least as effective as 25% at green....

10% of elderly, wealthy, yellow Boomers will have at least the impact that the 25% of young green Boomers did....

(Green is the highest value-meme in the "first tier" of development, stereotypically manifesting as an anti-hierarchical, politically correct, pluralistically valued self. Yellow is the lowest of the "second-tier" stages; in it, "[d]ifferences and pluralities can be integrated into interdependent, natural flows" [Wilber, 2000f].)

If 10% of the population one day reaches yellow, however, and if yellow is approximately *ten times* more efficient than green, then the 10% of the population at yellow would be approximately *four times* as effective, not merely *at least* as effective, as the 25% of the population at green (10 * 10%/25% = 4).

Further, if kw's presumption that Y = 10G were correct, then the *current* 2% at Y would already be almost as effective as the 25% at G. That is, if 2% of the North American population is currently at yellow, and 20% to 25% (kw's own numbers) is currently at green, and if yellow is "ten times more efficient" than green, then Y and G should be nearly of *equal strength* (20 vs. 20-to-25,

from ballpark figures to begin with) right now, in terms of their
influence on our culture.

Thus, minimal comparison of Wilber's claims against reality,
there, shows that things don't work at all, in practice, the way he
imagines they should. For, by his own testimony, it is the "greens"
who hold far more sway over politically correct academia than the
yellow-and-above, second-tier (or higher) leaders such as himself.
That position goes back at least to the early nineties, as kw indicates in the Preface to the second edition of his (2000) *Sex, Ecology,
Spirituality*. There, he relates that his attempted writing of a
"textbook of psychology" was cramped by the fact that the words
"development, hierarchy, transcendental [and] universal" were "no
longer allowed in academic discourse," owing to the "extreme postmodernism," "pluralistic relativism," and (green-meme) anti-hier-
archy attitudes which had supposedly spread through the academic world. As he put it in a related interview:

> [T]he green-meme dominates virtually all of conventional
> academia AND countercultural academia (Shambhala,
> 2001).

From untenable mathematics, to "responses from critics" who
are actually supporters: In *Boomeritis,* on page 244, kw has the
Powell character state:

> *The Shadow University: The Betrayal of Liberty on America's
> Campuses,* by Kors and Silverglate, is a thorough survey of
> the actual state of affairs. Far from being right-wing ideo-
> logues, its authors are liberals in good standing. Instead of
> quoting case after case—I urge all of you to consult this book
> for yourselves—I will give a few of the responses from critics,
> simply to try to convey a sense of the urgency and outrage.

"Powell" goes on to rattle off a group of very flattering quotes
from Linda Chavez, Alan Dershowitz, Christina Sommers, Nat
Hentoff, and Wendy Kaminer, in support of Kors and Silverglate's
book.

It turns out, though, that those supposed "responses from critics" are actually blurbs taken *ver batim* from the hardcover edition
of *The Shadow University.*

As every author knows, such blurbs are generated by individuals whom one already knows to be, or at least hopes to be,

sympathetic to one's ideas; they do not come from "critics." (Dershowitz, Hentoff and Kaminer were all actually thanked for their "assistance" by the authors in the front matter of the book.)

Granted, *Boomeritis* is purportedly a work of fiction—just as the rest of Wilber's writings are ostensibly based in fact. So, technically, he is allowed (in the former) to make up whatever "facts" he likes, and present them as if they were real. Unfortunately, there no way for the reader to tell which of the claims in that novel are meant to be taken seriously. Worse, as we have seen and will see much more of, Wilber's "real" research suffers from exactly the same penchant for "making things up out of thin air" as does his "fiction."

## CHAPTER IV

# INTEGRAL
# MEDITATION

IN 1999, WILBER PUBLISHED *The Marriage of Sense and Soul,* on the integration of science and meditation-based religion. That relatively error-free book actually received a complimentary review (Minerd, 2000) in the monthly *Skeptical Inquirer* magazine. Indeed, Minerd closed his evaluation with the generous comment that Wilber's writing was "refreshingly free of the pontifications, careless generalizations, and self-admiration indulged in by other writers." He also opined that "devotees of Wilber ... would be a group of people that skeptics could, if not quite embrace, at least live alongside very easily."

Surprisingly, Wilber actually quotes approvingly from Martin Gardner, regarding the Anthropic Principle, in that same book. So, contrary to what one might reasonably assume from the rest of his work, he does at least realize that the skeptical position exists, even if entirely disrespecting it in practice.

Thankfully, Minerd did note disapprovingly that Wilber "implicitly accepts the reality of mystical experiences, and it is sufficient for him that his scientific mystics test their internal experiences against nothing more than each other's internal experiences.

How this would eliminate group bias or error is not discussed." I have yet to find that obvious and *devastating* point addressed by Wilber himself anywhere in his own writings, before or since that review.

Interestingly, comparably flawed arguments as Wilber's, in favor of the "scientific" nature of meditation-based religion, were put forth by Itzhak Bentov in the 1970s:

> I am lucky to have met several people whose [meditative] experiences have been similar to mine, so that I have been able to compare my information with theirs. To my great surprise, our experiences agreed not only in general, but also in many unexpected details. This knowledge appears, therefore, to be consistent and *reproducible*.

(Wilber elsewhere [1982] quotes from other published aspects of Bentov's work. It is therefore likely that he was aware of the earlier [1977] book from which the above quote is drawn. Or, if he wasn't, as the "foremost theoretician in transpersonal psychology" he certainly should have been.)

Yet, the Nobel Prize-winning physicist Richard Feynman (1989) more reasonably noted:

> [T]he imagination that things are real does not represent true *reality*. If you see golden globes, or something, several times, and they talk to you during your hallucination and tell you they are another intelligence, it doesn't *mean* they're another intelligence; it just means that you have had this particular hallucination.

Further, a shared delusion, based on a common self-fulfilling expectation of experiencing "talking golden globes" or otherwise, is obviously no more real than is a hallucination confined to a single individual.

Wilber's vaunted "community verification," in practice within any closed environment, actually amounts to little more than an appeal to popularity and conformity. For, you can only be a "success" within those walls by seeing what the guru-figure and his "more spiritually advanced" (than you) disciples tell you that you should be glimpsing. Even the *external* experience of loyal followers seeing "miraculous coronas" (in guru Adi Da's community, for example) and the like, while skeptics were reportedly demoted for not seeing/imagining the same, has proved exactly that.

> Sound objective research is not relevant to the true believer. In place of evidence and scientific validity, things are said to work ... by using social pressures to persuade people that they did work; i.e., by gradually interfering with the individual's ability to evaluate information (Penny, 1993).

If the same purported sages were actually able to prove their claimed abilities to see auras, do verifiable astral remote-viewing or manifest objective coronas, for example, in a properly controlled environment, one might have *some* basis for confidence in the reality of their other internal experiences, even if those subtler experiences were not otherwise scientifically testable. (There is, after all, no *a priori* reason why everything should be "scientifically testable," in the physical laboratory or otherwise, in order to be "real.") But short of that, Wilber's hope that any amount of community verification might sort fact from fiction in mystical claims falls flat on its face. For, there are clearly no controls whatsoever in place to guard against meditators simply experiencing what they *expect* to experience, and then viewing that as a confirmation of the truth of the metaphysical theory previously taught to them.

Without a satisfactory demonstration of the reality of such spiritual experiences, integral "Theories of Everything" might as well be theories of leprechauns, unicorns and Santa Claus. That is, one struggles to find more certain truth-value in them than in, say, Tolkien's Middle Earth. Impressive monuments to human imagination, to be sure; but hardly deserving of being taken seriously as mirrors of "authentic spirituality."

That is so, particularly when the authors of the same wide-ranging integral ideas can be conclusively shown to have misunderstood and misrepresented so many of the established fields on which they base their "cutting edge" theories. Indeed, that would be a huge problem even were it not for the fact that the transpersonal data set, which they are creating their theories to explain, could hardly be more uncertain, i.e., as to which elements of it (if any) are valid, and which are spurious. Thus, even when reasoning clearly from that bad data, they end up effectively producing airtight arguments to prove how many integral angels can dance on the head of a pin, etc.—without having first bothered to properly ascertain whether such angels, and their auras and subtle energies, even exist.

Nathaniel Branden has given his own (partial) critique of Wilber's transpersonal methodology in his (1999) *The Art of Living Consciously*. (Note that Branden explicitly considers kw to be "one of the most brilliant men I know." So, he can hardly be viewed as being biased against Wilber.)

> [L]et us ask: Why should we believe the mystics' claims? On what grounds? Why should we even continue the discussion?
>
> To this inquiry, Wilber mounts an interesting answer. It is given in his book *Eye to Eye,* which is an attempt to justify the validity of knowledge attained through "the eye of contemplation," the mystic's alleged tool of cognition....
>
> [T]he process, we are told again and again, is in principle exactly the same as that by which one becomes a qualified scientist: knowledge is confirmed or disconfirmed according to whether qualified colleagues, having gone through the same steps, do or do not arrive at the same result. Experiments that are not reproducible or that do not yield the same results cannot be claimed to have revealed authentic truths. Therefore, in his or her own domain, the mystic's assertion of knowledge is fully as reliable as the scientist's....
>
> In other words, it is *reasonable* to accept the truth of such [mystical] insights. *Reason is still conceded to be the final arbiter.* "It is logical to accept these nonlogical, nonrational insights because...."
>
> That **I regard the argument as fallacious** is not my point here. My point is that, if one argues at all, there is no escape from using and counting on the very faculty mystics profess to have evolved "beyond." And this is the ultimate dilemma of anyone who is too conscientious simply to proclaim "It's true because I feel it."
>
> We may not always arrive at our insights by a process of reason, but reason is the means by which we ultimately verify them—by what is sometimes called "reality testing"—that is, integrating them into the rest of our knowledge and observations without contradictions....
>
> So what are we left with? A collection of assertions [by mystics, including Wilber himself] about the ultimate nature of existence that are riddled with contradictions, defy reason and logic, convey no intelligible meaning, invalidate our consciousness, destroy our concept of reality—and that we are

meant to take seriously while being told our limited development makes it impossible for us to understand them. If
one does not have an intellectual inferiority complex and is
not easily intimidated, this is not impressive.

Further with regard to the purported value of meditation in
one's own development, in Wilber's (2000a) *One Taste* journals he
states:

> We now have abundant evidence that meditation does not al-
> ter or change the basic stages of the development of con-
> sciousness, but it does remarkably accelerate that develop-
> ment. Meditation speeds up evolution. It accelerates the re-
> membering and the re-discovery of the Spirit that you eter-
> nally are. Meditation quickens the rate that acorns grow into
> oaks, that humans grow into God.

The closest that Wilber comes, in any of his books, to providing
any actual evidence to support such claims is in his (1998) *The Eye
of Spirit:*

> [U]nlike most of the meditation teachers in this country,
> [Charles N. "Skip"] Alexander and his colleagues have been
> taking standard test of the various developmental lines (in-
> cluding Loevinger's ego development, Kohlberg's moral de-
> velopment, tests of capacity for intimacy, altruism, and so
> on) and applying them to populations of meditators, with ex-
> tremely significant and telling results. The importance of
> this line of research is simply incalculable.

Yet, the endnote associated with that same set of complimentary statements offers these significant caveats:

> This is not to overlook what appear to be some valid criti-
> cisms of some of the TM® research [e.g., as performed by
> Skip Alexander], including occasional bias in the research-
> ers, inadequate methodology, and obliviousness to negative
> effects on practitioners. But even when those inadequacies
> are taken into account, what's left of the research is still
> quite impressive.

One might have hoped that such highly relevant information
would be featured prominently in the text, rather than being con-
signed to a tiny-font endnote. Such "valid criticisms" and "inade-

quacies"—i.e., red flags such as "occasional bias in the researchers, inadequate methodology, and obliviousness to negative effects on practitioners"—after all, might well be sufficiently disturbing for one to reasonably reject Alexander's Transcendental Meditation®-based research altogether. (Indeed, given Wilber's willing acceptance of aspects of that research which he wants to believe, one cannot help but wonder how much worse the methodology would have had to be before it was worthy of rejection. Knowing the dismally low standards of proof in transpersonal and integral psychology, one can only assume: "A lot.")

Further, regarding the admitted "negative effects on practitioners" of meditation: Would a prominent warning about that not have been merely ethical, given Wilber's continuing encouragement to others to take up meditative practice, even to the point of presenting that practice as a "moral imperative"? It is difficult to give voluntary informed consent, after all, when information is being withheld from oneself by persons whom one trusts to at least get that much right.

Interestingly, the CD and audio cassette programs of kw's (2003c) *Kosmic Consciousness* talks contain the following phrase: "I mention Skip Alexander who was a real genius and a real pioneer in this, and I still recommend looking into his work." That seven-second phrase, however, has been skillfully deleted from the online audio sample of the same program available on the Sounds True website.

Wilber continues, in the same audio program:

> [I]f you take people who are [raising kids and making money] and they meditate about an hour a day, then about four years later, they're **two stages higher** on any scale that we give them. Meditation is the only thing that's been empirically demonstrated to vertically move people to that degree.

That would be impressive if it were true. But the only evidence which kw ever gives of such claims comes, again, from the endnotes in *The Eye of Spirit,* where we read:

> For example, 1 percent of a college control sample scored at Loevinger's highest two stages (autonomous and integrated), whereas in a similar sample of regular meditators, 38 percent reached those stages....

That 38 percent broke through this ceiling with meditation is quite extraordinary. Moreover, if the Loevinger test is
slightly modified to be more sensitive to those at the higher
stages, 87 percent in one meditating population broke the
conscientious barrier, with 36 percent scoring autonomous
and 29 percent integrated. Alexander et al. (1990), p. 333.

Wilber's exposition then leaves one wondering: Does the original research describe an experimental methodology whereby people are tested to establish a baseline, then they meditate an hour a
day for four years, then they are re-tested and found to be one or
two levels higher? And was that done against a control group, who
did no meditation? (Or, even better, to account for the influence of
"expectation effects" in the test group, were members of the control
group given an "anti-meditation" technique—such as pacing and
focusing on problems—but told that it was a "meditation" which
would have the same anticipated effects of psychological growth?)
And were the members of the test and the control group randomly
assigned from the pool of subjects?

Short of such an adequate methodology, Wilber's own description of Alexander's studies indicates only that people at the highest
stages of Loevinger's scale of ego development tend to meditate,
not that meditation is what caused them to be in those high stages.
That is a correlation, at best, not a cause-effect relationship; it
could just as well be that independent evolution to the highest
stages of Loevinger's scale of ego development was what caused the
same people to begin meditating, or that something else caused
people to both grow/evolve/develop to the highest stages of Loevinger's scale and to meditate.

Even if kw (and Alexander himself) hasn't confused correlation with causation, though—and we will see shortly that they
*have* thus confused things—he is still basing an awful lot of the
practical side of his "integral religion" on a few *admittedly flawed*
studies. As a basis for either a science or a philosophy, that is a
miserably inadequate approach. Further, even if all of that were to
turn out to be valid—and even if meditation, in spite of its frequent
negative side-effects (to be detailed later), were to measurably advance one's psychological evolution—there is still no necessary
paranormal claim to any of it. That is, it still does nothing to sub-
stantiate the purported reality of the transpersonal levels of Wilber's four quadrants.

If one actually makes the effort to wade through the relevant chapter in Alexander and Langer's *Higher Stages of Human Development,* past the 40+ pages of "Vedic theory" and respectful references to the Maharishi's "seven levels of consciousness," one finally reaches the Research Appendix. There, all of the details of Alexander's "solid and ... repeated" research (in Wilber's unduly optimistic evaluation) are revealed.

Thus, from pages 331-2 of Alexander's book:

In two samples (total $n = 90$) of maximum security prisoners followed over a **one-year** period, both long-term and new TM subjects significantly improved by **one step** on ego development in comparison to wait-list controls, **dropouts**, and those not interested in learning TM (controlling for pretest scores and demographic covariates). None of the four other treatment groups followed longitudinally [i.e., over the passage of time] changed significantly on this measure (Alexander, 1982). On the average, regular new meditators (who scored at a concrete operational level at pretest) improved from the "conformist" stage of ego development (corresponding to dominance of concrete thinking) to the "self-aware" level (corresponding to the onset of reflective functioning of the intellect); and regular advanced meditators shifted from the self-aware level to a "conscientious" stage (corresponding to a mature form of abstract reflection).

This advance of **one step** for the new meditators over **a year** period substantially exceeds that for college students over a **four-year** period (Loevinger et al., 1985), yet at an age (26–29 years) and education level (ninth grade) where such changes are unlikely to occur. **Assuming** [!] that the advanced TM subjects started at a comparable ego level to the new TM group, they advanced a mean of **two steps** during less than three years.

So that is presumably where Wilber has gotten his "four years" and "two stages" information from, in his *Kosmic Consciousness* claim that "if you take people ... and they meditate about an hour a day, then about four years later, they're two stages higher on any scale we give them."

The problem with Wilber's presentation of that research, though, is that unless he has some other (unidentified) source for those claims, he is conflating several different studies into one—

and that latter study, as he presents it, was never actually performed:

- The prisoners in Alexander's study did TM for *one* year, not four

- From their one year of meditation, Alexander's subjects stage-grew by *one* step (in comparison to the control group), not two

- The college students in Loevinger's 1985 study were indeed tested over a four-year period ... but they were not meditating as part of the study. (If any of them were doing other forms of meditation on their own, that is just one more uncontrolled uncertainty in that second supposed "control" group)

Even if Alexander's prison-inmate subject study had otherwise been unassailable, it at most showed a one-step (not two) improvement in the psychological stage-development of its subjects over a period of one year (not four). Wilber's "two steps" are based on an *assumption*, explicitly stated as such by Alexander, which may or may not be valid. Yet kw presents it, either foolishly or dishonestly, as if it had actually been inarguably proved in controlled studies. It is an *assumption* which is potentially open to all kinds of selection biases, etc.

You cannot tell from Alexander's summarized write-up how the "new meditators" were chosen from the prison population. It is unlikely, at any rate, that the group was selected randomly from the inmates. In fact, since the study had a group of subjects who were "not interested in learning TM," there was an inherent selection bias in its protocol. Comparing that *self-selected* group (minus its dropouts!) to Loevinger's *randomly-selected* population (from a completely different study), by saying that "our meditators advanced more in one year than your normal students did in four," is just about nonsensical. It certainly has none of the scientific validity which kw presents it as having. (Amazingly, that prison study was Alexander's 1982 doctoral dissertation at Harvard.)

If Alexander had at least taken the self-selected prisoners who "wanted to learn TM," and split them into one group which was given the "real mantras," and another which was given fake or anti-meditation techniques, any measured differences between those two groups would have been impressive. As it stands, what he has done is just plain foolish, both in his own study and in the comparison to Loevinger's competently executed work.

Plus, Alexander's research was all done on practitioners of Transcendental Meditation. The results *might* well generalize to other forms of meditation, but one cannot merely assume, as Wilber does, that they will thus generalize.

Further, again from kw's *Kosmic Consciousness* talks:

> Another way to measure [the value of meditation] is to take the number of people that are at a particular stage of development in a particular development line like Jane Loevinger, and in her case, what she would call our level six, our integral level on our seven-level generic scale, she finds about 2 percent of the population reaches that stage. And after **four years** of meditation, **38 percent** of people doing it reach that stage.

And from *The Eye of Spirit:*

> That 38 percent broke through this ceiling with meditation is quite extraordinary. Moreover, if the Loevinger test is slightly modified to be more sensitive to those at the higher stages, **87 percent** in one meditating population broke the conscientious barrier, with 36 percent scoring autonomous and 29 percent integrated. Alexander et al. (1990), p. 333.

*But:* It was *eleven* years of meditation, not *four,* that got 38 percent of Alexander's subjects to test at the autonomous/integrated level! From pages 332-3 of Alexander's book:

> A longitudinal study ... compared change in ego development over an **11-year** period in graduates from Maharishi International University (MIU), where the TM program is incorporated into the college curriculum, to change in graduates from three well-known universities offering standard curricula.... From the pool of respondents from each of the control universities, students were matched as closely as possible with MIU graduates on gender, pretest age, and college class (i.e., cohort group). All subjects (total $n = 136$) were at least 19 years of age at pretest during the late 1970s. Most MIU graduates were currently regular in TM practice; most control subjects also indicated that they currently practiced some form of self-development, stress-management, or exer-

cise program for promoting physical and mental health (although none practiced TM)....

Whereas at pretest 9 percent of the MIU sample scored at Loevinger's higher "autonomous" and "integrated" stages, at posttest **38 percent** reached these two highest stages.

So, when Wilber says that four years of meditation got 38 percent of subjects to the "integral level," that's just plain false, from a man who cannot even quote the protocols from a simple longitudinal study accurately.

(Likewise, ten years of TM practice underlay the study that had 87 percent scoring above the conscientious level. Page 333 of Alexander's book makes that explicit.)

In the "38 percent" study, too, the meditators were self-selected, even though later being "matched up" (thus, potential rater/selection bias) against their control peers. So, that group went from 9 percent of them being autonomous/integrated to 38 percent of them being at those levels, while the control group had only 1 percent at those "two highest stages at both pretest and posttest." In a total of a mere 136 subjects from MIU and three control universities.

Even if there had been no selection or rater bias involved there, having only 136 total subjects means that exactly one person in the control group was at autonomous/integrated before, and after, the testing. So, there we have inadequately small study sizes for measuring states of development that are rare to begin with.

Further, consider that people on the verge of breaking through to the higher levels, or those having an explicit interest in and expectation for psychological growth, etc., might well choose to meditate and/or enroll in MIU from that cause, thus introducing a non-causal correlation between meditation and psychological stage-growth as the study proceeded. (Such interests and expectations can affect one's performance on written tests of maturity, too. That is, expectation effects apply to those tests, even if expectations themselves don't create psychological stage-growth. Loevinger had to explicitly take that into account in planning the testing for her 1985 study. Alexander evidently has not proceeded with the same professional care.)

Given all that, Alexander's studies, so valued and unduly praised by Wilber, have proved *nothing*.

The growth from 9 percent to 38 percent may well be causative rather than a mere correlation; who knows? But with Alexander's shoddy selection protocols and otherwise, a four-fold growth from 1 percent to 4 percent in their "control" group could have been just as significant, and meant exactly the same thing. For the sample size used (i.e., a control group of around 65, presumably), that growth from 1 percent to 4 percent represents just a *couple of people* in the control group breaking through.

So there are issues there, not merely with regard to protocol, but even just in terms of basic statistical significance.

And, note that 9 percent of the final 38 percent *were already at the integral level* when the study began. Assuming that there was no measurable regression of the subjects' levels in that study, then as far as *growth* to that level goes: Only 38% − 9% = 27% of the subjects *grew* to the integral level, of the 100% − 9% = 91% who weren't already at it. That is, only 27/91 = 32% who weren't *already* "spiritually evolved" managed to *grow* to the integral level. Over a period of *eleven years*. Conversely, 68 percent didn't experience the same growth, via meditation.

And that's supposed to be (in Wilber's words) the "doorway to God"? Something that (even neglecting all of the serious problems in the protocol) only works in any significant way for one-third of the people, over a period of more than a decade of regular practice?

And for the two-thirds who did not thus grow, what might they have done productively with their lives in the hours which they had otherwise devoted to meditation? What have they lost, in sitting and chanting nonsense-syllables to themselves?

Interestingly, the above-mentioned study by Jane Loevinger, et al. (1985) showed female university students demonstrating a "slight but consistent loss" of ego development from their freshman to their senior years. That loss, in turn, "challenges one assumption of a widely accepted version of Piagetian theory (i.e., that stage development is irreversible)."

Conversely, though, as Loevinger notes, "Piaget can hardly be cited for the frequent assumption that moral or ego development occurs according to a strict stage sequence, rarely admitting of backsliding. In his study of the development of moral judgment, Piaget (1932) went out of his way to reiterate that there are no strict stages. Even with respect to capacity for formal operations, Piaget (1972) warned of backsliding in young adults outside their own specialties."

(Wilber [1996] actually admits that such regression can occur, as does Alexander. KW, however, qualifies [via Stanislav Grof] the causes of that regression by saying that "under intense stress, or with certain types of meditation, or certain drugs, the self can regress to this [lowest] fulcrum and relive its various subphases and traumas, which tends to alleviate the pathology." None of those factors, of course, have anything to do with being outside of one's formop specialties. Nor was the regression found in Loevinger's study merely a short-term, coping response to "intense stress," etc.)

Obviously, if one can backslide from formop even just for being outside of one's specialties, attempting to correlate such stages of psychological development with three other quadrants (objective, cultural and social), as Wilber does, would scarcely be possible. That is so even were there widespread agreement in the field of development psychology as to the validity of Piaget's stages (which, as Meyerhoff earlier pointed out for us, there is not).

Of further interest, Loevinger notes that dormitory/fraternity/sorority life has been found to have a "constricting rather than a liberalizing effect with respect particularly to critical thinking," and thus to one's higher scoring on measures of psychological maturity. The worst possible combination for encouraging psychological growth, then, would surely be to live in a fraternity-like residence under a leader who can ostensibly do no wrong.

Ashrams, monasteries, and even integral institutes surely meet that criterion. Because even without living in residence in the latter, you cannot deeply question the "spiritually advanced" leaders if you hope to remain a member in good standing in the community. Rather, use your own mind in that environment to think critically about what you're being fed, and you will very quickly be demoted to the status of pariah, as we shall see.

As critics of the Ayn Rand cult have noted, "when people identify too closely with their system of beliefs, they have no choice but defend them tooth and nail from any hint of cognitive dissonance." That applies to integral beliefs and heroes just as surely as it does to Rand's Objectivist ones. It applies to groups of skeptics and scientists, too, except that the proper application of the scientific method works to eventually sort fact from fiction, limiting the length of time through which one can fool oneself.

Never forget that when Max Planck spoke of new ideas in science being accepted not for any logic of persuasion but simply for the older generation dying out and being replaced by a new group who had grown up with the more-radical view of reality, he was not talking about religious believers being unable to think clearly. Rather, he was directing that observation toward the supposedly rational *scientific community* itself.

In Wilber's (1999) response to John Heron's "not even wrong" (as Wolfgang Pauli would say, quite rightly) critique of his theories, he again pretended: "[O]ne study showed that, among individuals who meditated for **several** years, an astonishing 38 percent reached those higher stages." (Of course, the study in question again actually covered *eleven* years, not merely "several.")

The astonishing thing there is that Wilber, in point #16 of that same response, actually referenced Michael Murphy, et al.'s (1997) *The Physical and Psychological Effects of Meditation*. So he knows very well—assuming that he has actually read that book, as opposed to having merely cited it without having assimilated it—how meditation, far from being the "doorway to God," can utterly destroy people's lives. For, in the final, "Negative Experiences" section in Chapter 4 of that book, we read:

> Long-term meditators reported the following percentages of adverse effects: antisocial behavior, 13.5%; anxiety, 9.0%; confusion, 7.2%; depression, 8.1%; emotional stability, 4.5%; frustration, 9.0%; physical and mental tension, 8.1%; procrastination, 7.2%; restlessness, 9.0%; suspiciousness, 6.3%; tolerance of others, 4.5%; and withdrawal, 7.2%....
>
> Ellis (1984) stated that meditation's greatest danger was its common connection with spirituality and antiscience. He said that it might encourage some individuals to become even more obsessive-compulsive than they had been and to dwell in a ruminative manner on trivia or nonessentials. He also noted that some of his clients had gone into "dissociative semi-trance states and upset themselves considerably by meditating"....
>
> Hassett (1978) reported that meditation can be harmful. Carrington (1977) observed that extensive meditation may induce symptoms that range in severity from insomnia to **psychotic manifestations with hallucinatory behavior.** Lazarus (1976) reported that psychiatric problems such as **severe depression and schizophrenic breakdown** may be precipitated by TM.... Glueck and Stroebel (1975) reported that two experimental subjects made independent suicide attempts in the first two days after beginning the TM program.

*That,* not claimed-but-utterly-unproven psychological stage-growth even over decades of practice, is what any group (integral or otherwise) that encourages you to meditate, for whatever reason, is really offering you. (Note: Personally, I have had nothing but good results from meditation. Other people have not been so fortunate.)

Of course Murphy, with his deep transpersonal and integral biases and affiliations, cannot resist trying to put a positive spin on all that:

> Though the rewards of contemplative practice can be great, they do not come easily.

So, if meditation is producing clinically psychotic behaviors in you, apparently you just have to "work harder" at it. (That is, of course, exactly the remedy which your teacher and peers will suggest. And to not go along with that *bad* advice is effectively to admit that you are not fit or ready for the "fast track to enlightenment.")

Fear not, though: according to Wilber in his *Kosmic Consciousness,* CD 8 Track 9, prayer may be as valuable as meditation for psycho-spiritual growth:

> **Interviewer**: So it's possible that [contemplative] prayer could move you up **two levels** in a similar way as meditation?
>
> **KW**: Yes, I believe, I absolutely believe that....
>
> [Transcendental Meditation] has one advantage in that it's such a lineage practice, so to speak, there's a morphogenic field around it, if you will, it's so well developed, that when people take up that practice, it has almost immediate effects. Other practices are harder to get into, they're more sort of difficult. Zen is very difficult to do right; you have to practice it really for months, or even years, to really get into it. But TM, really within the first couple of sessions, you're really kind of getting the hang of it [so] it's an ideal type of meditation for research, because there's a similarity in people that practice it ... you can actually learn something by looking at people who do it. And people who do it for a very long time get into some of these very profound states, including twenty-four-hour-a-day subtle constant consciousness....

Would "contemplative prayer ... show the same stage-movement as the other types of meditation"? It probably would, keeping in mind that:

- The "research on meditation moving two stages" doesn't actually exist, but is apparently rather just the product of Wilber conflating a number of different studies by Alexander, none of which were done with anything resembling proper protocols in the first place

- Former accredited *teachers* of TM, who can certainly do the exercises properly, have been among its most vociferous critics (cf. www.suggestibility.org)

- The "profound states" which Wilber mentions, including the simultaneous existence of alpha and delta rhythms in the brain, even *if* that has been measured exactly as kw gives it, present no parapsychological or transpersonal claim or proof. Rather, it can just as well be simply an untapped ability of the "purely physical" brain, with or without interior feelings having an ontological reality on top of that. The same thing applies for Witnessing consciousness in general: resting in That, with the internal feeling that one has "no boundaries," doesn't even remotely mean that one really *is* infinite in consciousness. (Comparably, subjective feelings of astral traveling do not mean that one really *is* doing that—i.e., doing it to the point of, say, being able to read a five-figure number off of a designated wall, which is how these things are easily and competently tested, and invariably found to not be what their imaginative proponents claim)

- Zen is many times more a "lineage practice" than is TM: Fifteen hundred years of lineage and practice, versus a few decades for any widespread use of Transcendental Meditation. (Obviously mantra yoga in general is much older. But it is Wilber who is focusing specifically on TM, here, and touting the benefits of its "lineage.") And how is counting or watching one's breaths in *zazen* more difficult to learn to do, and make progress with, than is internally chanting a mantra?

So yes, prayer is likely just as (in)effective as meditation. Indeed, it is probably even a better option, as it doesn't have the range of psychotic side-effects which meditation tends to have.

Either way, though, Wilber's claim that meditation leads regularly to measurable psychological stage-growth is no more supportable than are his ideas on the "science of meditation."

None of those realities, however, have had any effect whatsoever on kw's claims for the purported transformative value of meditation, even as made in his (2006e) *Integral Spirituality:*

> [M]editation can help move you *an average of two vertical stages* in four years.

In the same book, Wilber repeated his self-serving but utterly false claims that "whereas around two percent of the adult population is at second tier, after four years of meditation, that two percent goes to 38 percent in the meditation group," and that proponents of Intelligent Design allegedly demand that "the Jehovah of Genesis" be the Eros driving the evolution of the Kosmos. All of those repeated untruths, of course, came from his pen well after the disproofs given herein were provided, online, even in his own Integral Naked forum.

CHAPTER V

# KOSMIC
# PARAPSYCHOLOGY

[Wilber] excoriates the suggestion of some New Age authors
that we can overcome any disease or hardship if our faith in
our own minds is strong enough; this claim, Wilber points
out, implies that it is our fault if we cannot cure our own cancer (Horgan, 2003a).

THE BELIEF THAT WE CAN "overcome any disease or hardship if our
faith in our own minds is strong enough," or via laying-on-of-hands
flows of healing energy from others, is indeed found throughout the
New Age community—even though no convincing scientific evidence of that possibility exists. And certainly, if either of those
abilities are anything more than imagination—or even if psychic
phenomena in general exist—there can be few if any limits to what
the human mind can do. Nor is such an attitude so far removed
from Wilber's own belief system as one might assume from the pre-
ceding quote:

Ken Wilber, as eager as he is to project a scientifically conservative image, once stated, "I'm sure [psychic phenomena] exist" (Horgan, 2003a).

Or, as kw himself elsewhere (1991) put it:

As I lay in bed, I noticed a series of subtle energy currents running through my body, which felt very much like the so-called kundalini energy, which, in Eastern religions, is said to be the energy of spiritual awakening, an energy that lies dormant, asleep, until aroused by an appropriate person or event.

In describing, to his second wife, his own experiences in a session with a laying-on-of-hands healer, he expounded further:

I could definitely feel the energy moving.... I think something actually does happen with gifted healers (Wilber, 1991).

If such energy flows exist, however, there is no reason why their intensity could not be increased by relevant practice, to affect oneself or others in both spiritual awakening and in *profound healing*, e.g., even of cancer. (Conversely, in the same view, a long-term restriction of such flows within one's own body could result in illness, as Brennan [1987] and many others have asserted.) Indeed, that increase is the very basis of the claimed temporary and partial transmission of enlightenment via *shaktipat* and *darshan* (i.e., the blessing which is said to flow from even the mere sight of a saint):

Since *shakti* is the divine energy, and since the guru is concerned with the transference of divine power, the use of that energy in such a transfer produces an immediate impact. That is *shaktipat*—the almost instantaneous transfer of divine energy, by touch or word or even look, from the guru to the [disciple] (Brent, 1972).

Further, with regard to the claimed power of the mind in healing, as the widely admired sage Aurobindo (1953)—one of Wilber's evident heroes—himself put it:

It is my experience and the [spiritual partner] Mother's that all illnesses pass through the subtle consciousness and subtle body before they enter the physical. If one is conscious, one can stop it entering the physical, one can develop the power to do so. We have done that millions of times.... Self-defense may become so strong that the body becomes practically immune as many yogis' are.

Incidentally, Wilber has been criticized, in Kazlev (2004) and Hemsell (2002), for having significantly misrepresented Aurobindo's philosophy in his (kw's) own writings; but that is a separate issue.

Wilber's second wife sadly died after a long battle with cancer, providing the context in which he was first confronted in a highly emotional way with often crassly applied New Age "blaming/responsibility" ideas regarding disease. (Having lost my own mother in the same way, I deeply sympathize with the suffering and support entailed.) He himself further weathered a mysterious, exhausting illness (RNase Enzyme Deficiency Disease, REDD) for several years in the mid-'80s, the long-term effects of which, as of 2002, again had him largely bedridden. He also suffered through the aforementioned six-month staph infection, in which he lost access to the always-already One Taste state. Those points are surely not irrelevant to his attitude toward the power of the mind with regard to cancer and other illnesses, as expressed above.

It is one thing to disparage New Agers for being "regressive" or "pre-rational" in their reliance on astrology, etc. But why be so bothered by them simply ascribing more power to the human mind in the potential for healing than you feel is appropriate? And if Wilber really has no tolerance for the "pre-rational" idea that we can heal our illnesses through the power of our own (or of others') minds and the associated/believed energy flows, why does he (2002) have his third (ex-)wife "doing industrial strength reiki" on him, in battling the effects of his REDD?

If the woman in question can truly direct the flow of subtle energies, or even if Wilber himself can genuinely feel those beyond mere imagination, there are any number of skeptical organizations throughout the world which offer significant monetary prizes for the simple proof of that. Short of their demonstrations of those claimed skills in a properly controlled environment, however, the *much* more likely explanation, for any betting man or woman, is that they are both simply imagining the beneficial effects of her "healings."

Of course, while insisting that "something actually does happen with gifted healers," Wilber has simultaneously disputed their interpretations of the effects of the subtle energies which they purport to be able to move. But if such healers can actually see auras and chakras, and move subtle energies, how could they so utterly misinterpret the results of their related attempted healings? For, those purported results would surely be visible *in exactly the same auras*. (Brennan [1993], for one, explicitly claims exactly that clear, unmistakable visibility.) Thus, there is precisely nothing that is open to "interpretation" in those healers' claims. Nor should one feel the least bit comfortable in accepting the existence of subtle energies simply for one's own easily fooled or imagined experience of those in non-double-blind environments, as is the case when kw vouches for their existence ... or touts (2005) the value of the Q-Link pendant for that matter, claiming:

> The Q-Link is a technology that amplifies and clarifies the body's energies. By reducing the noise in any energy field, this technology strengthens and purifies the body's own energies.

Beyond that, Wilber's aforementioned excoriating of New Age believers for their innocent position on healing cannot be meant simply to "spiritually awaken them." On the contrary, their denigrated view simply demands more responsibility than he evidently wishes to ascribe to human actions—including his own and those of his late wife. Indeed, that belief in the power of the mind, whether valid or not, is no more (and no less) pre-rational or magical than is kw's own acceptance of psychic phenomena, and his own acknowledged (even if merely imagined) perception of subtle energy flows, from claimed healers and otherwise.

Wilber's second wife actually entertained similar ideas to these (with regard to responsibility), at a point where she felt that he was blaming her for his lack of interest, at that time, in book writing:

> [H]e may not want to feel responsible himself, it might be easier for him to think it's [my] fault. What might be behind that? Maybe he's afraid it's his fault. Maybe he doesn't want to take responsibility for his not writing....
>
> Later that day I checked this scenario out with Ken, but very gently, no blame. He gave me a gold star, I hit it pretty close on the nose (in Wilber, 1991).

In any case, such patterns of behavior as Wilber admitted to his own late wife never confine themselves to any one aspect or incident in a person's life. Rather, they shape all aspects of one's existence, whether or not one is consciously aware of that.

Of myth and magic, now, kw (2000b) has stated:

> Unless otherwise indicated, when I use the word "mythic" it refers to preformal, concrete-literal mythic images and symbols, some aspects of which are in fact imbued with cognitive inadequacies, for these myths claim as empirical fact many things that can be empirically disproved—e.g., the volcano erupts because it is personally mad at you; the clouds move because they are following you. These preformal mythic beliefs, scholars from Piaget to Joseph Campbell have noted, are always egocentrically focused and literally/concretely believed.

Consider, then, Wilber's (1991; italics added) own attitude toward the possible effect of his second wife's death on the weather, where 115 mph gale-force winds beat the surrounding area at exactly the point of her passing:

> The winds, *I suppose,* were coincidence. Nonetheless, the constant rattling and shaking of the house simply added to the feeling that something unearthly was happening. I remember trying to go back to sleep, but the house was rattling so hard I got up and put some blankets around the windows in the bedroom, fearing they would shatter. I finally drifted off, thinking, "Treya is dying, nothing is permanent, everything is empty, Treya is dying...."

That, as a simple reporting of facts, is fine. However, years later, in his (2000a) journals, Wilber "coincidentally" reprinted a letter he received from the spouse of a hospitalized, terminal cancer sufferer, who had been touched by Treya's story:

> As [my wife] died in the afternoon a great storm and strong rain came up. And I saw a great grey cloud going upstairs from her body and drifting away out of the opened window. After twenty minutes the storm was over.

It is difficult to imagine Wilber including *that specific letter* in his reprints without it being implicitly in support of a "cosmic" nature to his own experiences. That is so even in spite of his previous "I suppose" (as opposed to a skeptical/rational "of course") regard for the "coincidental" nature of the winds blowing during his wife's death. After all, with the "great storm and strong rain" being explicitly associated with a "great grey cloud" rising from the dying person's body in the fan-letter case, could it really have been just coincidence for a similar storm to have arisen in his own wife's death? (If Wilber thought that that grey cloud and accompanying storm were pre-rational nonsense, he need not have included them in his own reprint of the letter. For, they are not at all essential to the man's story.)

If Wilber's winds were real parapsychological phenomena, beyond mere coincidence or imagination, that would mean that real magic exists, in the ability of human thoughts, intentions and/or emotions (i.e., subtle bodies) to affect the physical world. And in that case, New Agers could not rationally be excoriated for believing in such things. Rather, they should then instead be celebrated for having "correctly" divined and appreciated that aspect of reality. (The fan's wife made no recorded claim to be highly realized, yet still purportedly manifested that windy "magic." Thus, such claimed phenomena could not be restricted here only to the powers supposedly possessed by "great Realizers," etc.)

Short of Treya's death actually having affected, via real magic, the same winds which blow not merely for Wilber but for all of us, his implicit view of that phenomenon

> is simply reflective of mythic and magical thinking. That's okay, but it's not rational and if Wilber were to critique his own episode he would see it (via his spectrum psychology paradigm) as being "immature" (less inclusive, less rational, etc.)....
>
> Thus when I said Wilber was being narcissistic in his analysis of those winds, I was using the very adjective that Wilber himself on several occasions has used to illustrate a pre/trans fallacy, a mistake where the New Ager or whomever in question sees something mystical when it was merely mythic, where someone sees something paranormal when it was merely normal (Lane, 1996).

Note that Lane insightfully spotted that point a full four years prior to Wilber's reprinting of the "grey cloud" fan letter.

In relation to all of the above paranormality, further consider the following recent perspective from Wilber (2003) himself, in expounding on the nature of the chakras in his "comprehensive theory of subtle energies":

> I will ... simply use one example: the overall summary of the chakras given by Hiroshi Motoyama.

Wilber then goes on to explain, for his own demonstrative purposes, Motoyama's standard and non-controversial "theories of the chakras," from his book of the same name. (Motoyama himself is founder and president of the California Institute for Human Science: www.cihs.edu.)

There is, however, much more to Motoyama's (2000) *Karma and Reincarnation* worldview than that:

> Ritual offerings of food and water are truly effective ways of helping beings suffering in the astral dimension, particularly the souls of people who have recently died. When we place an offering upon the altar, we don't expect it to disappear because we know that someone who has died cannot eat physical substances. When we expand our field of vision into the higher dimensions, however, we can actually see spirits consuming the offerings. They are consuming the "ki" [i.e., the *chi* or *prana*] of the food and water, the astral energy of the objects that exists even before the object manifests into the physical world.

One assumes that Wilber would not himself endorse these latter claims—of spirits eating subtle energy, etc. If not, however, *why not?* If Motoyama's clairvoyant perceptions of the chakras are taken as valid, why would his comparable perceptions, *through the same subtle senses,* of ghosts and astral gods not be taken as equally valid? Did he see the chakras validly and clearly, but hallucinate everything else? If not, how can you justify "picking and choosing" only what you want to believe from those perceptions?

Of course, if such phenomena as Motoyama describes really do exist, a lot of what Wilber denigrates as being "pre-rational" or the product of regressive magical or mythical thought would again not be so. Rather, it would instead be appealing to aspects of reality which simply do not fit into his own theories. That point would apply specifically to sacrifices to nature spirits or to human ghosts

who could *very conceivably* actually be "personally mad at you."
Indeed, Motoyama (2000) describes exactly such appeased ghostly
anger in the very same book, along with his psychic interactions
with water and tree spirits:

> Yoichi had been dead for 800 years, yet his tortured spirit
> was still able to affect me when I began to build our retreat
> center. We began to pray for his soul in the Shrine. After
> three years of such prayers, his resentment dissolved and I
> no longer experienced any negativity.

> I could see that the Spirit of the tree was grieving about its
> impending doom.

> I saw that the Water Spirit was understandably outraged
> and was retaliating by causing the family its present prob-
> lems.

It is no large step from tree and water spirits to volcano and
cloud spirits; if the former were to exist, surely the latter would,
too. And according to Motoyama, the former do indeed exist, as
surely (or unsurely) as do the chakras which in turn figure into
Wilber's theories of psychological/spiritual development and subtle
energy.

Stepping further out from there into the New Age, then, Wilber (2003b) has bravely conjectured:

> Internality is the form of spacetime's self-prehension, a self-
> organization through self-transcendence (to put it in dry
> third-person terms), or—in first-person terms much more ac-
> curate—the love that moves the sun and other stars.

Interestingly, the tail end of the above block quote is actually
taken, without attribution, from Dante's *Divine Comedy*. The overall block itself comes from a series of excerpts from a forthcoming
planned book in Wilber's "Kosmos" trilogy, the first installment of
which was his *Sex, Ecology, Spirituality*—"one of the most significant books ever published," according to Larry Dossey.

From Part 4 of that same online "Excerpt G":

> The major theorists addressed [in my "comprehensive theory
> of subtle energies"] include Rupert Sheldrake, Michael Mur-
> phy, William Tiller ... Deepak Chopra, Hiroshi Motoyama,

Marilyn Schlitz, Larry Dossey, and Gary Schwartz, among others. I am a great fan of all of those theorists, and much of this integral theory has been developed over the years in discussion with many of them.

Corresponding to his unfounded belief in subtle energies, paranormal winds, and the abilities of the above "theorists," Wilber has given the impression of believing that the infamous "Maharishi Effect" is real. From page 433 of *Boomeritis,* with the Jonathan character speaking:

> There is a very large body of empirical evidence showing that when 1 percent of the population of a town, say, begins to meditate, then crime statistics all go down sharply. Murder, rape, theft, they all go down. It's called "the Maharishi [E]ffect," and **even skeptics admit that it's a real phenomenon**.

"Even skeptics admit that it's a real phenomenon"? Pure nonsense! Skeptics *do not* regard the "Maharishi Effect" as being a real phenomenon. James Randi, in fact, had given a debunking of that purported effect as early as 1982, in his *Flim-Flam!* Martin Gardner, likewise, in 1995 dismissed the Maharishi Effect as being "supported, of course, by highly dubious statistics." (Members of the Maharishi's university, though, have given their own [Rainforth, 2000] "detailed rebuttal" to at least one critique of their "voodoo science.")

Randi and Gardner were voted as being the *top two* "outstanding skeptics" of the twentieth century, in the very same issue of *Skeptical Inquirer* where Wilber's *Marriage of Sense and Soul* was given an unduly tolerant review.

If you want to know how little Wilber's name and work are respected in the skeptical community even now, consider this: In the autumn of 2001, I attempted to interest Randi in testing Wilber's own (2000a) claims, of being able to stop his brainwaves at will. I simultaneously informed him that kw was considered to be "at the top of his professional field." I also let him know that Wilber had served on the same Board of Editors of *The Journal of Transpersonal Psychology* as does Stanley Krippner, with whom James works regularly. (Krippner actually wrote the foreword for Rothberg's anthology, *Ken Wilber in Dialogue.*)

Randi responded tersely that he had "never even heard of" kw, and expressed his disdain at the prospect of having to "chase after" Wilber (and after the claimed spiritual healer Barbara Ann Brennan, of whom he had equally not heard). That response was given even while Randi was simultaneously and explicitly "chasing after" *many* others, with regard to their potential participation in his million-dollar Paranormal Challenge. The clear implication there was that, given Randi's own high position in the skeptical world, if Wilber were anyone of note, Randi would already be familiar with his work.

Of course, since kw's aforementioned book was again reviewed in the very same "outstanding skeptics" issue of *SI* in which Randi was voted as the #1 skeptic of the twentieth century, chances are rather amazingly good that James *had* actually at least heard of Wilber's work, even if later having that fact slip his mind. Brennan, too, has been mentioned briefly in other issues (e.g., Park, 1997) of the same magazine. And yes, however absurd it may be, both Wilber and Brennan are indeed widely regarded as being at the top of their respective "professional" fields by their peers.

Stumbling further into parapsychology, we find Wilber making the following claims in his (2001d) CD, *Speaking Of Everything:*

> **KW**: U.C. Irvine had been given, I don't know, a $500,000 dollar grant or something to do another series of psychic research.... And I said basically that I think that was a misuse of money. Because the real problem is that we have meta-analysis on psychic phenomena....
>
> **E.com**: Yeah, Dean Radin's book [*The Conscious Universe*]. It's fabulous.
>
> **KW**: That's right. It puts it **beyond dispute**, and **every statistician agrees**. So I said take your $500,000 and buy a fucking P.R. firm.
>
> **E.com**: Right.
>
> **KW**: Because you people **just have bad press**. Another experiment is not going to change. It's already **one hundred percent certain**.

One can, however, easily locate a *statistical* refutation of Radin's analysis, by Ray Hyman and J. McCrone, at *The Skeptic's Dictionary* (Carroll, 2005a). The conclusions which follow from it refer to exactly the same book which kw regards as being unassailable:

> Based on the results of these experiments, Radin claims that "researchers have produced persuasive, consistent, replicated evidence that mental intention is associated with the behavior of ... physical systems" (Radin 1997: 144). That sounds like a hasty conclusion to me. He also claims that "the experimental results are not likely due to chance, selective reporting, poor experimental design, only a few individuals, or only a few experimenters" (Radin 1997: 144). He's probably right **except** for the bit about it being unlikely that **the experimental results are due to chance**.

And note how, at that same skepdic.com page, all of the papers quoted to refute Radin's 1987 meta-analysis claims were published *prior* to Dean's own (1997) book.

Where, then, did Wilber get the confidently presented but brutally untenable idea that Radin's work was actually valid, much less inarguably so? Why, from text in Radin's own book, of course, as quoted on the enlightenment.com website:

> "Informed opinion even among skeptics, shows that virtually all the past skeptical arguments against psi have dissolved in the face of overwhelming positive evidence," and "informed skeptics today agree that chance is no longer a viable explanation for the result obtained in psi experiments."

Note how the already indefensible "informed skeptics today agree" from Radin becomes the even worse "every statistician agrees" when processed through kw's view of reality. (Presumably Radin was referring there to ostensible "skeptics" like the people at www.skepticalinvestigations.org ... including himself.)

Here is how one cogent reader of James Randi's (2002) column suggested competently testing the Q-Link pendant which Wilber is likewise convinced has real effects:

> First, a volunteer not communicating with the tester takes ten Q-Link devices and ten dummy devices, which are identical, but have been disabled. The volunteer makes a list of numbers from 1 to 20 and randomly numbers the devices, keeping track of which is which. Now, someone else chooses any 10 of these 20 units and takes them to our friend Her-

bert. His job is to separate the good ones from the phonies. If what he claims is true, he should be able to use a subject (or ten separate ones) and determine, without fail, which are which. With ten units, he has a one-in-1024 probability of getting them all right by chance. And I'll bet a case of premium tofu that he can't do it!

On the other hand, Wilber's (2001d) standards of "proof" for the Q-Link go this way:

[T]he amount of scientific evidence on [the Q-Link] so far is small, but very, very promising. You've seen some of it on TV, and stuff.

Just how comfortably is Wilber ensconced with the makers of these new "technologies"? As he himself notes in his (2003) "Excerpt G":

Any good model open up lines of further research, and the integral or AQAL model is no exception. I have been developing many of these research agendas in conjunction with Bob Richards, co-founder of Clarus, Inc. [maker of the Q-Link] and a **vice president of Integral Institute.** We would be glad to discuss these issues with interested parties.

Richards is also on the Advisory Board for the Chopra Foundation, headed by Deepak Chopra.

CHAPTER VI

# WILBERIAN
# MATHEMATICS

WE ALL LEARNED AND APPLIED the Pythagorean theorem in high school, in a form very closely resembling the following:

> The sum of the squares of the lengths of the sides of a right-angle triangle is equal to the square of the length of the hypotenuse.

Wilber's own (1996) infamous version of the same principle, however, instead reads like this:

> [T]he sum of the squares of a right triangle is equal to the sum of the squares of the hypotenuse.

It is clear what Wilber is *trying* to say there, but only because we all learned the theorem itself in high school—his actual statement is meaningless nonsense. (Succeeding editions of the book have, of course, corrected that text at the start of its Chapter 13.)

Interestingly, the *real* Einstein worked out his own, innovative proof of exactly the Pythagorean theorem ... *at age twelve*. Of course, Albert also managed to be viewed, nearly universally and in spite of his poorer private behaviors, as a "Jewish saint," rather than an "arrogant asshole" (Wilber on himself, in [Horgan, 2003a]). He further did that without resorting to unconvincing false modesty, and even while doing unparalleled work as a *real* genius. There is a lesson in there somewhere. It is, indeed, a lesson in remaining humble and subject to correction, not simply by one's awed and overly respectful peers, but rather *in the face of truth.*

Significantly, then, Albert's most frequent answer to questions put to him in public, on wide-ranging issues which he was, by his own admission, not sufficiently informed to be certain of his opinions, never entailed an attempt to oracularly bluff his way through in order to maintain his status as an "Einstein." Rather, his most frequent response was simply, and admirably, "I don't know."

By contrast, to sustain the feeling that one is a contemporary genius even amid wholly embarrassingly missteps and misrepresentations of *high-school-level ideas* cannot be easy, from any psychological perspective.

Despite the "Pythagorean Fiasco," Wilber is currently in the process of developing his own (root) branch of mathematics—an "integral calculus of indigenous perspectives":

> As far as I can tell, this primordial mathematics appears to be the root mathematics from which all others are abstracted abstractions [*sic*] (Wilber, 2003b).

Well, perhaps. More likely not, in my opinion, but *perhaps.*

In any case, one cannot help but wish the man well in his "new branch of mathematics" endeavor—in which he is currently all of "3% done."

And perhaps, given his history, light a candle.

CHAPTER VII

# INTEGRAL POLITICS

AT A RECENT WORLD ECONOMIC FORUM, Bill Clinton (2006) referred complimentarily to Wilber's (2001b) *A Theory of Everything,* saying:

> "[T]he problem is the world needs to be more integrated but it requires a consciousness that's way up here, and an ability to see beyond the differences among us...."

KW himself, interestingly, had earlier given his own defense of the Clintons' interest in transpersonal ideas, in his (2000a) *One Taste:*

> The cautionary tale. Michael [Lerner] is friends with Bill and Hillary, and his "politics of meaning" was particularly espoused by Hillary. The liberal media found out about it [in 1996] and had a field day. Saint Hillary, Michael was "Hillary's guru," and so on.... A simple visualization technique [taught by Jean Houston], used by thousands of therapists daily, was turned into Hillary's "channeling" Eleanor Roosevelt, whereas all she was doing was creative visualization. But anything *interior* is so utterly, radically, hideously alien

to the liberal media that they could hardly discuss the topic without snickering or choking.

Yet, in 1983, Curtis D. MacDougall, emeritus professor of journalism at Northwestern University, had written an entire book detailing the attitude evinced by the very same "liberal media" toward gurus, clairvoyance, ESP, and various less "interior" spiritual pursuits (e.g., astrology, ghosts, witchcraft and UFOs). From that back-cover copy:

> In *Superstition and the Press,* America's most distinguished journalism professor and veteran newspaperman provides a devastating critique of the treatment by the press of claims of supernatural phenomena. This book documents virtually every story about paranormal events to appear in American newspapers for more than a generation. The author's conclusion is that newspapers, with rare exceptions, treat claims of supernatural experiences and paranormal phenomena without questioning their validity.

Further, Al Franken observed, in his (2003) *Lies and the Lying Liars Who Tell Them:*

> The right-wing media tells us constantly that the problem with the mainstream media is that it has a liberal bias. I don't think it does. [Sullivan (2005), however, quotes research done at UCLA which proves that there is indeed such a predictable left-wing bias.] But there are other, far more important, biases in the mainstream media than liberal or conservative ones. Most of these biases stem from something called "the profit motive."

James Randi (2003) has likewise noted:

> Educated mainly in the humanities, thus lacking hard scientific training or savvy, and with the constant goal of finding the "perfect story" always applied to their backs, [the media] snatches at any and all scraps of propaganda that filter down to them from the heights above [i.e., from purported "real psychics"], gratefully embellishing and flavoring them before presenting them to the consumers below, in return for appropriate tribute, of course....
>
> I've mentioned before the fact that the dozens of tests of power-of-prayer that are carried out every year, often at

great cost, only produce a fraction of positive results, well within the expected range of error—but those are the results—the only results—that media editors choose to feature.

And from Jacqueline Deval, in her (2008) marketing guide, *Publicize Your Book!*:

> The reporter's job ... is to get a good story for their readers. They are looking for angles in everything you say and do.

Read even just a little bit into the skeptical perspective and you will find that, to the present day, skeptics are at least as disgusted with the overly credulous nature of media coverage of claimed paranormal phenomena as Wilber is with the same media for not being credulous enough!

The reality is that any informed and unbiased presentation of the various transpersonal claims eagerly accepted by kw would be "bad press." And the more informed and fair the presentation was, the worse it would be for him and his ilk.

Venturing further into "integral politics," Wilber (2003d) has predictably given his opinion on the war in Iraq:

> I personally believe that any protest movement that does not *equally* protest *both* America's invasion *and* Saddam's murder of 400,000 people is a protest movement that does not truly represent peace or non-aggression or worldcentric values.
>
> I am aware of no major protest movement that has protested both forms of violence equally, and that has insisted upon an immediate end to both aggressions, **and offered a believable way that both aggressions could actually be halted immediately** so that neither side can continue its homicidal actions.
>
> That is, I am aware of no integral protest movement anywhere in the world, unfortunately.

Amnesty International is a "major protest movement." While not officially condemning the war in Iraq, to any right-of-center political perspective they have done much more to "harm" the American cause there than to aid it:

> Critics of AI have suggested that AI's concern for the human rights implications of this war disproportionately criticize

the effects of U.S. military action while in comparison they were less vociferous about the abuses of the Hussein regime and the human rights implications of the continued rule of this government (Wikipedia, 2006).

And yet—

Supporters of AI have pointed out that AI was critical of Hussein's regime while Donald Rumsfeld was shaking the Iraqi leader by the hand, and that when the White House later released reports on the human rights record of Hussein, they depended almost entirely on AI documents that the U.S. had ignored when Iraq was a U.S. ally in the 1980s.

Indeed, "the September/October 1988 [Amnesty International] newsletter's lead article was an appeal to the United Nations Security Council to 'act immediately to stop the massacre of Kurdish civilians by Iraqi forces' under Saddam Hussein."

Wilber might try to hide behind the idea that AI hasn't protested those two sets of evils *exactly* equally—which, by definition, it couldn't have, regardless of which side it might (or might not) have favored. (Plus, in not officially taking a stand against the Iraq war, AI has obviously explicitly protested it far *less* than they have objected to the tortures and mass murders under Saddam's rule. So, evidently, in order to show themselves to be properly integral, they should be protesting it *more,* odd as that may sound given their mission and history.) Amnesty also probably never had a plan to offer in which "both aggressions [i.e., the invasion of Iraq, vs. Saddam's mass murders] could actually be halted immediately." Did *you?* Did *kw?* Not likely.

By Wilber's own absurd third criterion of needing to have presented such a plan in order to qualify as "integral" in his judgment, he fails as miserably as anyone: Not only is there no movement which meets that third standard—a quite unnecessary one, in terms of evaluating one's good intentions or state/stage of consciousness—there is probably not even a single *individual* who does. (If there was a workable and obviously correct political solution to that problem, which kept everyone honest in the process, Bush would never have gotten away with that rushed invasion in the first place.)

So why does kw even bother framing all that? Why does he set it up so that, in practical terms, no movement could possibly be "integral" with regard to the Iraq conflict ... even while he himself and his institute are "integral" by definition?

My strong suspicion? He is doing it to reserve high integrality only for meditative beings such as himself, regardless of how superior the behavior of others may be in practice when compared to his own ideas and character.

If you disagree, consider kw's self-aggrandizing (2000a) statement, in *One Taste,* that "until the ecologists understand that the ozone hole, pollution, and toxic wastes are all completely part of the Original Self, they will never gain enlightened awareness, **which alone knows how to proceed** with these pressing problems." There, too, he is basically integral by definition, even though being less than ecologically conscious in practice (i.e., for his leather couches and Thanksgiving turkey dinners, whatever one may otherwise think of such things).

That Wilber would have ever put the above "ozone" ruminations into print, without considering how blatantly self-celebrating and openly grandiose they are, smacks of something far worse than a mere occasional "mental lapse." And again: Where is *his* workable, integral solution to the ecological crisis? Nowhere, even for ostensibly having an "enlightened, integral awareness" in his own consciousness.

Given all that, it is no surprise that any other movement, such as Amnesty, composed merely of "ordinary mortals," must be "nonintegral" ... until its members (who obviously overlap significantly with the ecological movement) attain to the same exalted state of consciousness as kw thinks he possesses.

Consider also the perspective of Greenpeace (2003)—*the* typical "green meme" organization, explicitly cited as such by kw (2000f) himself—in outlining their reasons for officially protesting the war in Iraq from the beginning:

> We don't support Saddam Hussein. We don't back any governments or political leaders. When we decided to take a stand against this war, it was because we see a far greater danger in the concept of preventive war....
>
> For one nation to take arms against another because it *believes* that nation to be a threat undermines the foundations of peaceful coexistence, multilateral institutions like the United Nations, and an "entire web of laws, treaties, or-

ganizations, and shared values," to quote John Brady Kies-
ling's letter of resignation from the U.S. diplomatic core.

As tempting as it may be to those who view Saddam as
a cipher of evil to step in and remove him militarily, one has
to ask what's next?

After the U.S. conducts a preventive war on Iraq, will it
set its sights on Iran? North Korea? And if the U.S. can wage
a preventive war to protect its national security, shouldn't
India or Pakistan have the same right?

This is the first step on a slippery slope. It ends with the
United Nations in tatters and the rule of might making
right.

If you are wondering how significantly the membership and
culture of Greenpeace overlaps with that of Amnesty, consider Rolf
Schwendter's (1991) explicit mention of those two groups in exactly
that context:

> Examples for the clusters and networks of pivot institutions
> [as gathering-points for members of overlapping cultures] ...
> would be groups like Amnesty International, Greenpeace,
> World Wildlife Fund—a large number of political, cultural,
> human rights-centered, ecological, self-help-oriented organi-
> zations.

The reactions exhibited by "patriotic" Westerners post-9/11
and immediately prior to the war in Iraq included the need for pro-
tection by a religious or political "savior," the witch-hunting eradi-
cation of "evil," and the willing surrender of one's freedoms in that
hunt. We further saw the voiced belief by American newsmen that
"we're winners," being attacked by "losers" only because of that
ostensible superiority; and the regarding of anyone who dared to
question the claims of the country's alternately lying and priority-
shifting leaders as being "unpatriotic." We also had death threats
against the likes of the courageous Dixie Chicks and the leaders of
Greenpeace, by persons who obviously identify so strongly with
their nationwide "cult" as being "the best in the world" that even
the suggestion that one could be embarrassed by the bullying behaviors of its leader(s), or that the evil "out there" might not be the
immediate threat which it is presented as being, causes them to
wish you dead.

It is therefore worth considering the fairly obvious point that both religion and politics utilize the same techniques of manipulation on their followers, bringing out *exactly* the same psychological defenses in their adherents. Does it really make a difference whether the Evil Other is Satan, or communism/terrorism? (If you studied Arthur Miller's play *The Crucible* back in high school, with its intended parallels between the Salem witch-hunts and McCarthyism, you already know that it makes no difference.) Could the psychological reactions/defenses really be any different against one than against the other? Isn't it *obvious* that, given a structurally comparable set of threats and fears in the political world as in the religious, the psychological reactions to those real or perceived dangers will likewise be hardly distinguishable?

Whether or not the dangers actually exist as presented by the leader/guru is secondary. To bring out the cult-follower defenses, it is enough that one *believes* they exist and that only the right guru/president/ideology can keep one's body and/or soul safe from them.

As the social psychologist Philip Zimbardo (2004b) then put it, after elucidating ten "ingredients"—from rationales for engaging, to small first steps, to high exit costs—for "getting ordinary people to do things they originally believe they would not" do:

> Such procedures are utilized across varied influence situations where those in authority want others to do their bidding, but know that few would engage in the "end game" final solution without first being properly prepared psychologically to do the "unthinkable." I would encourage readers to do the thought exercise of applying these compliance principles to the tactics used by the Bush administration to get Americans to endorse going to war against Iraq.

Robert J. Lifton (2003) likewise noted the inclination of America's leaders "to instill fear in their people as a means of enlisting them for illusory military efforts at world hegemony." One need not agree with the latter half of that reading to recognize the penchant of a nation's people to periodically and obediently rally 'round the flag, even when it was obvious that they were being deliberately manipulated.

Yet, there are always persons who are subjected to exactly the same attempts at coercion and subtly enforced obedience, and yet who have enough ability to think for themselves that they are able to see through the attempted manipulations, and refuse to go along with the lies of the political, spiritual and "integral" leaders, even if doing so gets them branded as unevolved (or unpatriotic), and thus not worthy of membership in the "saved" group.

CHAPTER VIII

# INTEGRAL
# CENSORSHIP

DR. CHRISTIAN DE QUINCEY (www.deepspirit.com) is a professor of philosophy at John F. Kennedy University in California. He is also the managing editor of the *IONS Review,* published by the Institute of Noetic Sciences. (IONS was in turn founded by astronaut Edgar Mitchell.) In late 2000, he published a critique of Wilber's integral philosophy and emotional character in the peer-reviewed *Journal of Consciousness Studies* (JCS).

Wilber (2001c) responded with over forty single-spaced pages of attempted demonstrations as to how de Quincey had misrepresented his work and his character.

De Quincey (2001) volleyed with a twenty-eight page "refutation of the refutation."

One of Wilber's students, Sean Hargens (2001)—also a member of the Integral Institute—then replied with fifty-plus pages of text to "refute the refutation of the refutation." In it, he simultaneously and reasonably asserted de Quincey's tendencies toward passive-aggressive behavior (in his writings), and reliance on pop psychology in his character analysis of Wilber's "nasty tone."

And there the matter has rested.

Until now.

It is not my purpose here to attempt to evaluate those authors' respective criticisms of one another. Rather, I would simply like to note several allegations which de Quincey has made regarding the behind-the-scenes aspects of the relevant processes. Those may then give one pause when considering the overall health of the consciousness-studies field. In particular, they may cast some additional doubt on the aspects of that field which closely surround Wilber and his followers, shaping as that proximity does the allowed discussions around them.

In commenting on how Wilber may have obtained pre-publication knowledge of the detailed contents of his original submitted paper, de Quincey (2001) has suggested:

> [Wilber's] friend Keith Thompson, evidently, had passed along a series of *private and confidential* email exchanges between Thompson and me. I had included Thompson in the group of prepublication reviewers, and had lengthy online conversations with him—particularly about I-I [i.e., intersubjectivity]. However, I explicitly prefaced our exchanges with a request that the contents of our conversations be kept confidential, and should not be shared. Thompson agreed, and said he would honor my request.
>
> Not only did he "approach" Wilber and "warn" him of "severe distortions," Thompson used the content of my emails to write a critique of my Wilber critique, which he sent off to JCS, suggesting that either his paper be published as a Wilber review instead of mine, or perhaps alongside mine. Not surprisingly, the JCS editor saw right through the ruse. Thompson took this underhand action without informing me, clearly breaching a confidential agreement between us. Very unprofessional. A clear case of "Wilber police" mentality. (Thompson, and his friend and Wilber acolyte Sean Hargens, later tried a similar tactic to suppress publication of another article on Wilber I'd written for *IONS Review!*)

Any devoted disciple would, of course, have behaved in the same way, in defending his guru-figure's "honor." That is, dissenting opinions are never allowed, and an (alleged) broken promise is a small price to pay for preserving the sage's public image.

Given all of the above, one further cannot help but wonder: Did Wilber himself know about those alleged attempts at suppression?

Recall: According to de Quincey, their mutual friend Keith Thompson was in contact with both of them after allegedly breaking his promise of confidentiality to de Quincey. He was also the same individual who reportedly suggested to JCS that they publish his analysis of Wilber's work, rather than de Quincey's review. Would Thompson have gone forward with that, without bouncing the idea off Wilber first?

If Wilber did know about Thompson's alleged plans, his acceptance of that way of doing things, even if that acceptance meant simply doing nothing to stop Thompson, would be absolutely chilling. The *real* Einstein, for one, would never have stooped to such poor behavior.

Ironically, Wilber (2000a) had earlier voiced his own attitude toward the need for a free exchange of ideas within the consciousness-studies marketplace and elsewhere. That was given in terms of the importance of passionately communicating your vision, Kierkegaard-like, regardless of whether you are right or wrong, that it might be heard and adjudicated by a reluctant world.

One wonders, though: Would Wilber and Keith Thompson allow de Quincey equally valid passion in speaking his own vision, without (Thompson allegedly) covertly attempting to stop the publication of the latter's disagreeable ideas?

Regardless, contrary to Wilber's impassioned but misled plea, being right *does* matter. For, being wrong only makes it more difficult for correct ideas to be heard above the prevailing cacophony. Everyone who has ever done fundamental, thrillingly original work in any field—e.g., Einstein, Bohm, Benoit Mandelbrot (via fractals), etc.—has discovered that the hard way. For, the established misunderstandings place literally decades of resistance into the path of the acceptance of right ideas. That Wilber has encountered far less "wailing and gnashing" of scholarly teeth speaks much more to the synthetic and frequently derivative nature of his own (esp. early) ideas than to anything else.

In my own case, regarding the "Wilber police," from the beginning of my published debunking of kw's false claims and consistently inadequate research, the most loyal members of his community have predictably reacted very negatively to being informed of the truth about his work.

Foremost among those "integral experts" and censors has been a follower employed as an "education analyst" in Wheaton, Illinois, going by the online name of Goethean. His (2005) response to my exposing of kw's indefensible support of the long-discredited claims of Intelligent Design boiled down to this:

> Geoffery [*sic*] Falk is an asshole who is not to be trusted on these matters whatsoever. His book, *Stripping the Gurus* proves on every page that he is out to gain fame for himself at the expense of those who are his superiors in every way. (He has samples online to prove it!) His words are pretty much irrelevant to any honest inquiry on any subject.

Since that same individual functions proudly as a self-appointed guardian of the Ken Wilber Wikipedia page, no one should be surprised to find that, for many months, he (and others) succeeded in blocking any mention of my debunking of Wilber from that public space, even when the relevant links to my work had been placed there by interested third parties with whom I have had no contact.

Immediately after my first attempt at getting those critiques listed on that Wikipedia page, Goethean went through all of my other attempted contributions to the debunking of other spiritual leaders on Wikipedia, removing any of them that hadn't already been deleted by other censors equal to himself. (Some of those pages already had links to Rick Ross's immensely valuable but grossly copyright-violating website [www.rickross.com], collecting the non-book-length exposés of numerous gurus and so-called cult leaders into a single database.) He had only an IP address to go on there, however, and so could not reasonably remove those links for being "self-promotional," given that the links were thus posted anonymously. Yet, that is exactly the reason which he gave for deleting many of them.

Goethean (2006) has since given the following extremely dubious justification for his censorial actions:

> I agree with User:Nofalk's assessment of the Geoffery [*sic*] Falk piece. I find it inappropriate for this page. It's an essay by someone with a deeply studied ignorance of Wilber's writings. It's inaccurate to call it a critique. To dismiss something out of hand without understanding it is not a critique. It's an unsympethetic [*sic*] dismissal. I had the link under that topic heading before the edit war started. There are

writers who believe that Wilber's influence on culture has been nothing but negative, and who eviscerate Wilber for what they percieve [sic] as fundamental theoretical errors. I can accept and even applaude [sic] those critiques, and will gladly link to them from the article and describe those critiques in the article. But Falk doesn't even make a small attempt to understand the work that he's criticizing. He's like a bumpkin looking at a Jackson Pollack [sic] saying "I don't know what art is, but that ain't it."

As usual in the Wilberian community, however, there is not even a hint given there as to how I have allegedly misunderstood kw's ideas; just the unsupportable smoke-screen assertion that I have.

Plus, in my first attempt (on August 25, 2005) at getting my critiques listed on the kw Wikipedia page, I had given links not only to my original "Norman Einstein" chapter (in STG) but also to the "Wilber and Bohm" appendix from this present book. That appendix was Ph.D.-endorsed, even before its online publication, as being "brilliant and deeply insightful." So, it would certainly qualify as a *critique* of Wilber's work, even if one could argue (wrongly) that negative analyses of his character have no place in an encyclopedia entry.

Of course, if it was up to "Truth-seekers" such as Goethean, nothing of the thoroughly researched work which I have done in exposing the lies and abuses perpetrated in the name of religion— whether integral or otherwise—by our world's spiritual authority figures would exist anywhere. As he notes (2006), with obvious satisfaction:

By the way, someone once tried to create a Wikipedia article about Falk's book, "Stripping the Gurus." After some research, it was deleted by the Wikipedia community (more of whom, it should be noted, are biased against Wilber, or have never heard of him, than are biased for him) on the grounds that the book was self-published on the [I]nternet and was not notable enough to merit an article. — goethean 16:43, 19 December 2005 (UTC)

In general, STG would offend anyone who wanted to believe in the set of fairy tales called religion/spirituality. So really, only agnostic and/or atheistic editors wouldn't have a personal reason to regard the book as not being "notable," and thus to expedite its removal.

Over three-quarters of the American population self-identifies as Christian (Adherents, 2005). Conversely, when less than 15% of the American people list themselves as having no religion, you are at risk of offending close to 90% of the population in speaking out against religion and spirituality in general. So, anyone can see that although the majority of the Wikipedia community/editors will not have even heard of Wilber, when 85% or more of the editors and community members are not going to in any way welcome hearing the truth about the associated abuses, delusions and manipulations in the spiritual world, it is built into the system that the text won't receive anything resembling a fair hearing.

Goethean's state of mind comes through clearly enough when he further says: "As someone else noted Dasein, you seem to have an axe to grind, care to share?" When even calm, reasoned dialog in support of alternative viewpoints is denigrated by self-appointed censors as arising only from one's ostensibly having "an axe to grind," you need not wonder why Wilber's community was viewed —even prior to his "planned meltdown" in July of 2006, the subject of the next chapter—by people who understand cult and in-group dynamics, as being on the verge of degenerating into a *bona fide* cult.

I am by no means the only cogent critic of kw to have run afoul of integral "experts" such as Goethean. First, as Chris Cowan (2006) observed in terms of the reception given to his version of Spiral Dynamics by the custodians of integral information:

> Our own small adventures with the Wiki world have demonstrated for us how the psychology and motivations of contributors can sway "truth" and their approach to its promotion. If there is a culture of open inquiry and sharing, things have a chance to work. If there are fanatics with agendas— either ideological or financial—or fixated minds stuck on particular ideas, then the outcomes turn into products of endurance, competitiveness, and alliance-building. If you've got a couple of folks who believe themselves without peer, it's a problem. And for those who find such things unpleasant or not worth the effort, truth inevitably suffers. It doesn't take but a couple of rotten apples to spoil an egalitarian barrel. There has to be a mechanism for rotating the fruits and monitoring process, as well as content.

Jeff Meyerhoff has predictably fared no better for his writing of a full-length (2006) book critiquing kw's ideas, entitled *Bald Ambition*. Rather, for that, he was subjected to the following absurd dismissal from Wilber and his colleagues:

> [S]ome critics aren't at the appropriate altitude to make cogent criticisms (Ken's example: Meyerhoff). Due to this difference in altitude, there is nothing you can say to satisfy such critics. You can, of course, always learn something from any criticism, but that's not the issue (Edwards, 2006).

Personally, I **couldn't disagree more** with such foolish denigrations of what is one of the few cogently argued and thorough criticisms of Wilber's work. And so I will quote extensively, below, from Meyerhoff's delightfully well-reasoned and well-researched text:

> Wilber presents his model as if the consensus of scientific opinion supports it, but this is not the case. By tracking down his sources, revealing in them what Wilber does not mention, and exploring more fully the disciplines he uses, I will show that Wilber's version of individual development is not a valid generalization of scientific findings....
>
> It is not only alternate sources that can be cited to contradict Wilber's assertion of scholarly consensus, his own sources when examined closely yield a different picture than the one he presents....
>
> Wilber now calls the basic levels of development waves and the lines of development streams, following the usage of Howard Gardner et al. in their 1990 article. He cites and quotes this article several times as evidence for his claims about the universality of the basic levels. And the parts of the article Wilber cites do support his contentions, but the quotes are carefully selected and a return to Gardner et al.'s article reveals evidence that runs counter to Wilber's model.

Even on other topics, the integral "facts" are no more accurately given:

> Wilber's unreliable reporting of the results of scholarly research is one central feature of my critique and this same problem arises, although less severely than usual, when he justifies vision-logic by citing scholarly research....

Wilber's characterization of the magic, mythic and rational stages often veers into caricature. This is because he makes facts fit a particular theoretical mold to preserve his theory.

Of course, if you are surprised by any of that, you have simply not been paying attention. Because it is all exactly what you would expect, just from knowing Wilber's history, back to his first steps in transpersonal psychology in the late 1970s.

Meyerhoff again:

The four quadrant map, as originally drawn in SES, depicted the four different aspects of each holon. Each holon had an individual, social, exterior and interior aspect. Yet Wilber routinely referred to individual and social holons, not individual and social aspects of holons.... Wilber's commentators have demonstrated in great detail how this semantic slip reveals what is crucially problematic about Wilber's four quadrant model, causing Andrew Smith to recently conclude "that the four-quadrant model, in its original form, is dead."

As Smith (2001) himself put it:

[T]he criteria that Wilber and Kofman provide for distinguishing individual and social holons are useless. Some of these criteria either fail to make the distinction at all—as shown by the fact that they apply to some of their listed examples of individual holons ("molecules, cells, organisms") as aptly as they do to social holons; others can't be applied at all.

Chapter 1, Section B of *Bald Ambition*, drawing heavily on Smith's excellent work, actually deconstructs Wilber's vaunted "twenty tenets" to such a devastating degree that there is practically nothing left in those supposedly universal principles to regard as being valid.

Amazing, isn't it? That the mess which kw has created in his "great breakthroughs" over the past three decades isn't even remotely logically consistent. ("Instead of having one map in which we fit three overlapping classifications—objects of inquiry, methods and validity claims—we actually have three which don't overlap. In addition, the distinctions which create each of these three maps don't stay in their respective categories.") And that is worthy of being called "philosophy," or even just "competent scholarship"?

> Wilber wants a duality in Plato's thinking to be the essential duality driving Western civilization; "the dualism of which all other Western dualisms are merely an incidental subset." To do that, the influence of Plato has to be inflated, hence the [dishonest] changes in Whitehead's aphorism [from "the European philosophic tradition consists of a series of footnotes to Plato," to encompass all of "Western civilization"]....
>
> Reardon's study [i.e., *Religion in the Age of Romanticism*] demonstrates how integral an ascendant spirituality or other-worldliness was to Romanticism's great interest in nature and history's this-worldliness. This directly contradicts Wilber's characterization of it as mired in "flatland ontology" (Meyerhoff, 2006).

More from Meyerhoff, in his (2006b) "What's Worthy of Inclusion?":

> Nonexclusion is [Wilber's] idea that differing fields of knowledge study differing phenomena in ways particular to their field, so that people outside the field, who study different phenomena with different methodologies, can't usefully comment on what goes on in another field.

But, as far as that ridiculously *ad hoc* principle of "nonexclusion" goes: If Wilber were to actually apply that idea, he would be the *first* one to be disqualified from having anything to say.

Plus: Could kw have come up with a better way of dismissing the criticisms against himself and his unsupportable ideas by people *outside the integral field?* That is, people who by definition "can't usefully comment on what goes on" there, for not having meditated until they hallucinated, etc. (Wilber's *Up from Eden* was based on a vision he once had of the spiritual-evolutionary unfolding of the kosmos, in ontogeny and phylogeny. That alone should have been a glaring red flag, regarding the man's inability to distinguish reality from his own fantasies/fabrications.)

Of course, Wilber *claims* (falsely) to be accurately representing the "agreed-upon-knowledge" in the fields which he includes in his four quadrants, thus conveniently giving himself a free pass on the difficulties of commenting on or evaluating areas in which he has no formal training and has made no recognized, peer-reviewed academic contributions. But, what happens, then, if you disagree with his frequently inaccurately given "orienting generalizations," executed on fields in which he has no more training than you do?

Meyerhoff has made additional insightful points, regarding Wilber and his community, in his (2006a) "Six Criticisms of Wilber's Integral Theory":

> Instead of the image of Wilber being confronted with a vast array of knowledge and fitting it together like a jigsaw puzzle, a more plausible explanation is that he already had a progressive, developmental, dialectical story of the Kosmos in mind and found, not the orienting generalizations of the sciences, but cherry-picked scholars who *appear* to validate the view he wants to be true.

It is actually much worse than that, though: Reading that fine collection of documented misrepresentations by kw, it again becomes obvious that he either has not understood (even at an undergraduate level) the basic knowledge in the fields which he purports to be synthesizing or, if he *has* understood it, he is unconscionably twisting/misrepresenting it to suit his "theories," and expecting to get away with that, for never having been properly critiqued by his peers in transpersonal psychology. (And, prior to 1996 or so, he really didn't get caught. So, the implicit confidence was actually quite justified.) *No competent, honest person could be as consistently wrong as Wilber is in (mis)representing other scholars' positions to make them appear as if they support his own.*

> There is a difference between, as it were, negligence, which is random in its effects, i.e., if you are a sloppy or bad [source of information], the mistakes you make will be all over the place. They will not actually support any particular point of view.... On the other hand, if all the mistakes are in the same direction in the support of a particular thesis, then I do not think that is mere negligence. I think that is a deliberate manipulation and deception (Richard Evans, in [Shermer, 2005]).

Wilber's mistakes are indeed always in support of his particular point of view. And for that, he has been subjected to a good amount of spicy criticism, from myself in particular.

That is hardly unfair to him, though: In the world of real science, Wolfgang Pauli, for one, was renowned for his scathing destructions of several ideas which, years later, went on to win Nobel Prizes. *That* is what you may expect to have directed your way if you venture into *real* fields of academia, even when bringing *valid* ideas into them which challenge the norm.

In the transpersonal and integral worlds, however, one finds more of a "covenant of lunatics," whereby it is implicitly agreed that, if I take *your* "imaginary friend" (i.e., spiritual experiences and theories) as being real, you will in turn take seriously my delusions and elevation of perfectly normal phenomena to the status of paranormality. And neither of us will ever properly criticize the other, because "it's all good."

If you find the existence of that implicit "covenant" and its effects difficult to accept, consider the following independent observation regarding the reasonably suggested causes of widespread contemporary prejudice against atheists: "It is possible that the increasing tolerance for religious diversity may have heightened awareness of religion itself as the basis for solidarity in American life and sharpened the boundary between believers and nonbelievers in our collective imagination" (American Atheists, 2006). That, of course, is exactly the same dynamic, even in a comparable context, except that instead of hallucinations and the like being a common bond worthy of mutual respect, we instead have belief in God and Morality. In both cases, though, religious tolerance and the death of reason (in not being allowed to point out the foolishness in others' irrational beliefs) go hand-in-hand, and are further accompanied by a blatant *intolerance* for and distrust of others outside of that covenant.

So, no surprise by now that one is indeed allowed to respectfully find small, "correctable" flaws in Wilber's work, and still remain a member in good standing of the integral world. But, uncover glaring and/or fatal shortcomings in the ideas, and provable incompetence and/or dishonesty in their creators' work and character, and what can you be but an "untrustworthy asshole"? Or at least, as Meyerhoff has experienced, be dismissed as "altitudinally challenged" in proportion to the strength of your arguments?

It is obvious (and completely predictable from basic human psychology) that the vast majority of Wilberians have no more interest than the average "good Christian" would in doing the "archaeology" of going back to the original sources upon which their respective systems of beliefs are based. Were they to do that, though, they would find that, just as the innocent mistakes and less-innocent influence of the personal theologies of ancient scribes created a "multitude of mistakes and intentional alterations" in ways that sometimes "profoundly affect religious doctrine" in the Bible, comparable distortions will occur even when the best of integral theorists are involved.

Of course, it is so much easier to simply believe what you are told, and to rely on the "community" to not allow members to rise into positions of respect without their ideas being valid, than to question (and research) everything, back to its original sources/languages. No surprise, then, that those psychological realities apply just as much to the "trans-rational" integral community as to the "pre-rational" Christian one, and produce a comparable milieu, with members of both in-groups imagining themselves to be reasoning clearly from established facts, when all they are actually doing is rationalizing hazily from a set of (ineptly and/or intentionally) distorted principles.

When Albert Einstein did his Ph.D. thesis, well after his "miracle year" of 1905, one of the reviewers returned it with a comment akin to, "I can't understand a word of what you've written here." More recently, Benoit Mandelbrot experienced a decades-long dismissal of his groundbreaking work with fractals.

That is what happens, though, when you trust the middling "community"—whether spiritual, scientific, or artistic—to be able to distinguish between genius and quackery, when by their very "average" nature they cannot. For, the unexceptional members of any community, while perhaps being able to recognize quackery, will tend to lump works of real genius into the same category, for not being in a position to evaluate them intelligently.

In addition to the analysis of kw's work by individuals such as Meyerhoff, Matthew Dallman (2005b) has given fascinating comments on the dysfunctionalities present in the Wilberian community. Dallman actually worked intensively as the volunteer art director for Integral University for sixteen months; he knows from whence he speaks. And thus doth he speak of "meanness, vitriol, nastiness, and insult directed by [kw] to myself and my wife."

Wilber's dismal treatment of Michel Bauwens (2004) is also worth noting:

I was ... privy, since I was in regular email contact back then, to Wilber's private denunciations of institutes like the California Institute of Integral Studies and the Naropa Institute, schools that I had monitored, visited, and have many highly qualitative [sic] teachers and researchers. It's not that he said that they were imperfect, no, they were "cesspools" and one would have to stay at all cost away from them. This aggressiveness I personally found disturbing. I started to notice how easily Ken praised works that favorably use his work, he did it with my own magazine *Wave,* which he highly praised in a note even though he could not possibly read the Dutch-language it was written in, while being so aggressive with those who disagree.

Finally, there was a personal incident. In short, I had sent Ken, whom I considered a friend by then, since I had visited him and interviewed him for four hours, a draft of an essay on the new world of work, which clearly stated that it was inspired by his work, specifically mentioned a series of consultants working in his spirit, then went on to describe the four quadrants, and apply them creatively to my own domain, with notes and references and all. I got back a letter which threatened me with "exclusion from the network" and even legal consequences for "intellectual theft."

One does not have to look hard at all to find, in Wilber's integral community, the reluctance to question his ideas, the marginalizing of anyone who does dare to debate his edicts, the paranoia which sees even cogent and completely reasonable questioning as an "attack," and the absence of dialogue with outside perspectives.

None of that, though, has been the product of any overwork or explicit coercion of its members, nor has there been an "escalating series of public commitments" required of the members to bind them to the ideology and community, nor is Wilber their "savior," etc. Rather, the mess there has evolved, even against the best intentions of the persons involved, via simple human nature. It is just a group of people defending their "specialness" and salvation, and the "genius" of their Hero, against other less-special "outsiders," while basking in the comfort of a sadly-false worldview in which "everything makes sense."

In a sense the members of the integral community could be viewed as having been "tricked" into believing a set of false ideas from Wilber himself. But 98% of them wouldn't have had it any other way. That is, if kw hadn't fed them what they desperately need to hear, with a veneer of science and rationality, they would have found someone else who would.

And so the environment develops in which doubters are branded as heretics, by whatever name, and good members are made to
feel so special for being "integral" or second tier, as opposed to the
"axis of non-integrality" outside, that they can't bear to leave the
community. For, that departure would equate to an admission of
failure in their "most important, prime directive" spiritual quest.

It would be intuitively plausible to say that the less sense
one's ideas make, the more they must be protected from questioning by competent outsiders. Wilber's ideas make dangerously little
sense, and he has been caught, red-handed, fabricating information far too often by now, for anyone of sound mind and body to
look past those deceptions and/or incompetencies as if they were
anything less than pandemic in his work. In fact, the only way he
will be able to preserve the "integral edifice" he has worked all his
adult life to create, against further disintegration, is by completely
closing it off from any cogent questioning.

So, what do you think he will be doing, in that regard, over the
next few years? What does the dismissal of Meyerhoff's delightfully
reasoned work—so well-thought-out, in general, that it goes right
over the heads of the vast majority of integral community members
—as being "altitudinally challenged" tell you about what the "integral" future holds?

Closed-society in-group dynamics, particularly when combined
with promises/expectations of enlightenment/salvation, have a way
of reducing both leaders and followers to behaving in the worst
pre-rational and conformist ways, regardless of how loftily they
may test or behave in "normal" circumstances. Compare the sadis-
tic/submissive behaviors in Philip Zimbardo's (2004) Stanford prison experiment, by persons who only qualified as subjects in the
first place for being the most psychologically healthy of the appli-
cants. Or, consider the aforementioned psychological regression
measured by Jane Loevinger in female university students—a
"slight but consistent loss" of ego development from their freshman
to their senior years.

Personally, I don't think that people need to be "tricked" into
joining destructive spiritual organizations, nor kept there via mind
control, to nearly the degree to which that idea is given currency in
the cult-studies world. But that simply means that I consider the
situation to be much *worse* than does the field in general, not that
mind control isn't practiced ... even at the hands of integral pandits. It *is* practiced, but most people will fall for the community's

claims and slip into unquestioning obedience even without that suppression of debate, or the like. Regardless, where you have mind control, you proportionately have a cultic environment.

In July of 2006, following Wilber's meltdown, I was contacted by the head of one of the major anti-Scientology websites, through another cult-studies professional, regarding his wish to meet personally with Wilber and "reality-test" him. He also said:

> We are going to cover your book [i.e., STG] in our next ... ezine. I and others will also carefully read the Wilbur [sic] work. After I have had some tome [sic] to read more of your work I would like to talk by phone on how we might feature some [of] it on [our] home page.
>
> We have 10,000 subscribers....

And that was the last I heard from him. Because, of course, when he/they actually read my Wilber-debunking work, he will have seen that I do not at all buy into the self-exonerating fiction—accepted gospel though it may be in the cult-studies field—that people who have wasted the best years of their lives in destructive groups were merely "brainwashed, innocent victims" of sophisticated, deliberate systems of mind control. (It will not have helped that the famous ex-Scientologist who made that offer—Lawrence Wollersheim, of FACTNet—is now the Co-Executive Director of the Integrative Spirituality [2007] group. The latter is in turn "largely inspired by Ken Wilber's integral philosophy and Don Beck's Spiral Dynamics" [Huston, 2005].)

It is well-known that members of closed, destructive groups tend to be idealistic persons. Well then, what do idealists do, if not elevate their heroes to positions of near-perfection? Rather than simply lamenting that so many well-meaning persons get involved with such "chosen" groups, why not recognize that the same idealism, and its oft-associated projection and narcissism (in the hope of changing/saving the world through one's membership in a special group of like-minded people), is a big part of what creates the problem in the first place? That, though, would require taking responsibility for one's own actions and gullibility rather than blaming others.

So, no surprise that even these well-known and highly respected anti-Scientologists, who are courageous enough when it comes to standing up to and exposing that organization, would rather ignore one of the few in-depth resources which thoroughly exposes kw for the grossly manipulative spiritual leader that he is, rather than face the most unflattering reasons for their own participation in our world's allegedly destructive groups. Much easier to cry about how they were manipulated to the point where they couldn't think for themselves (!) than to admit their own deep desire to be told pleasant salvational lies by "perfect" authority-figures. They assert more or less out of thin air that, without having been subjected to one or another form of "mind control," supposedly no one would ever believe that one or another alternative spiritual leader is what he claims to be ... and follow that up by vouching for "safe, traditional" religions which invariably not only began as full-blown destructive cults, but which have teachings which are every bit as nonsensical as the best of L. Ron Hubbard's spiritual fiction.

They will even absolve the inner circle surrounding the guru/pandit from any responsibility for their actions in abusing others, as those high members, too, were allegedly under the same "mind control"; thus leaving only the guru-figure, among thousands or millions of "innocent victims," to be painted with any blame for the utterly predictably, social psychology-based nature of the community. How oddly convenient, in that it further absolves these experts for *their own* abuses of peons while holding inner-circle positions in their respective groups.

And those are the same people who make the rules about what you are allowed to think and theorize in cult studies, and still be accepted as a knowledgeable professional there: If you want to be a member in good standing of that biased and heavily religious/spiritual group, and not be guilty of blaming the victim, you had better not question the most sensitive aspects of their accepted wisdom too deeply, regardless of how *obviously* one-sided and even outright wrong it may be.

Cult members, more often than not, are simply "religion addicts" who would believe absolutely *anything* that got them into a "saved" group (where any overt attempts at mind control, though those most certainly do exist, are almost overkill):

> Addiction is not a disease but rather a habitual response and
> a source of gratification and security that can be understood
> only in the context of social relationships and experiences....
> Addiction is characterized by the repeated use of substances
> or behaviors despite clear evidence of morbidity secondary to
> such use.... Addiction is often applied to compulsive behav-
> iors other than drug use, such as overeating or gambling....

In all cases, the term addiction describes a chronic pattern of behavior that continues and is perceived to be hard or impossible to quit at any time....

Addiction is often characterized by an ongoing effort to use more (drug or behavior), tolerance, and withdrawal symptoms in the absence of the stimulus. Many drugs and behaviors that provide either pleasure or relief from pain pose a risk of addiction or dependency....

Instead of an actual physiological dependence on a drug, such as heroin, psychological addiction usually develops out of habits that relieve symptoms of loneliness or anxiety. As the drug [or behavior] is indulged, it becomes associated with the release of pleasure-inducing endorphins, and a cycle is started that is similar to physiological addiction. This cycle is often very difficult to break (Wikipedia, 2006c).

Members of established religions and of smaller guru/pandit-led groups clearly suffer from an excessive need for social sanction for their beliefs, a tendency to elevate people they admire to "infallible hero" status, a strong desire for acceptance from their then-great heroes, and a deep need to belong to a "saved" in-group. The psychological comfort (and yes, endorphins) which one's meeting of each of those needs confers is common to both groups, in equal measure.

Conversely, whether you are one of Jehovah's "Chosen People" or one of Sun Myung Moon's comparable selected few obviously makes no difference in terms of the psychological dynamics involved in that feeling of "specialness." Likewise, you may be safe in an ashram from the demonic *maya* outside; safe in the Catholic Church from the influence of Satan "out there," at least so long as you confess your every mortal sin (including masturbation) on a regular basis; safe in Jonestown from the planted "snipers" in the surrounding jungle; or safe in a "second-tier" institution from the "attacks" of the purported 98% of the world which is "first tier"— and which supposedly cannot, even in principle, understand you, until its ("Mean Green Meme") members evolve to your own high perspective. In all of those cases, you will have the same need for a "safe sanctuary," even if the intensity of fear you feel at those mostly-imagined "persecutions"—and the corresponding degree of "protective" closure of the community from outside influences and questioning—may differ.

The organization may be led by a living guru/pandit or by a deceased one; that difference matters little in either of those (specialness and felt safety) regards.

Cult leaders, if they deign to formulate theories as to what a cult is, will invariably set up those criteria so that their own group isn't at risk of being categorized as a cult—being either blind to their own abusive manipulations, or deliberately overlooking or suppressing those. In exactly the same way, the leaders in cult studies cannot bring themselves to admit that the same weaknesses which made them susceptible to becoming psychologically "trapped" in one or another recognized cult are also what brought them back to the "safe" religions of their respective childhoods (e.g., the Roman Catholic Church, with its "safe and normal" history of Inquisitions, murderous Crusades, and witch-hunts).

Cult-studies professionals further typically emphasize how persons will get involved with destructive groups at low and vulnerable points in their lives, neglecting to note how the need for meaning in life can be felt just as strongly when one is "on top of the world," and yet still finds that there is something missing.

Regardless, when such persons "escape" from one or another closed, destructive community, to be free to believe whatever they want, and then choose to believe that they are still one of the Chosen People, or that Jesus and Mary are everything they're claimed to be in salvational terms, they have just exchanged one set of fairy tales for another. Such people are psychologically "addicted" to religion every bit as much as are others who flit from guru to guru to pandit.

If religion (even in its "alternative" forms) is indeed the opiate of the masses, it comes complete with its own existential, social and biological (re: endorphins) withdrawal symptoms, to keep you hooked—all of which is basically implied even just by Voltaire's statement that if God (and "perfect gurus") didn't exist, we would (and do) create them. "Even if my present guru turns out to have feet of clay, the next one will be the real thing"; even if all the religions I've been a member of are false, there is a true one out there somewhere, etc.

And, since the guru nearly always frames himself as being the source of all the good feelings one initially had in his presence, and as being the divinely ordained channel for all bliss-experiences and enlightenment, there is powerful incentive to keep going back for more, even if getting your hits from a different "dealer." (And if you don't think that meditation, like drugs, can function as a form of escapism, think again.)

Perhaps one in a thousand guru-figures uses his/her power wisely and non-abusively. Ken Wilber, for all his glaring flaws as both a pretend-scholar and a desperately insecure human being who will brook no criticism of his ideas without attempting to discredit the "enemy" as being too spiritually unevolved to understand his Great Notions, has never been the worst among those "leading" figures. Rather, he is simply the one who makes the most quantitative statements. And thus, he is also the one who can be the most easily shown to be consistently wrong and/or dishonest, via simple research which any intelligent undergraduate should be able to do.

Nevertheless, it is easy to underestimate the degree of psychological abuse which goes on in even "neutral" or "moderate" groups such as the Integral Institute, where you "can leave any time you want" without the threat of physical violence being used against you for doing so. If you think, then, that the "freedom to disengage" makes such depression- and suicide-inducing "spiritual prisons" safe, or in any way easy to leave, you really need to put *much* more thought into the subject.

You can start with pondering how even Wilber (1991) himself, at the low point of his second marriage, went out gun-shopping, intending to end his life rather than just walk away from that sorrow:

> I will walk into Andy's Sporting Goods, on Park Street in South Lake Tahoe, to buy a gun meant to vaporize this entire state of affairs. Because, as they always say, I can simply stand it no longer.

CHAPTER IX

# BALD NARCISSISM

A few years ago, a book honoring Wilber, *Ken Wilber in Dialogue,* collected the views of many ... critics, allowing Wilber to engage them all. But I found it illuminating that he did not concede a single substantive point to any of these critics, and that he identified a single writer out of them [i.e., his close friend Roger Walsh] whom he felt completely understood his system—the only writer who made no real criticisms of his system at all (Smith, 2004).

[T]he believers of a purported synthesis [by Wilber] will have to work overtime and employ a great deal of cognitive dissonance not to see the facts and theories that don't fit into their integral embrace (Meyerhoff, 2006).

ON JUNE 8 OF 2006, Ken Wilber posted a very revealing entry on his blog, exhibiting something of a "Wyatt Earp" complex. That is, as an underappreciated gunslinger/sheriff/savior, out to save the Wild West according to his own version of the Kosmic Law. From that embarrassing rant:

> In short, it's just ridiculous to say that I try to hide from this criticism, I live on it!.... This is what second tier does automatically anyway, it takes new truths wherever it finds them and weaves them into larger tapestries. It can't help doing so! If I find one, I am ecstatic! So mark this well: Only a first-tier mentality would even think that one would run away from good criticism.

Wilber, however, does indeed run away from competent, thorough criticism like vampires flee from the sunlight. Mark that well. You do not need to be first-, second-, or nth-tier to see that; all you need to be able to do is recognize competent research when you see it, and then note kw's derogatory response to (or freezing-out of) that. You will not find anything resembling the same academic competence in Wilber's own writings, which is exactly why he needs to so hysterically marginalize people who can think and research far more clearly and thoroughly than he has ever been able to do.

If you read that full rant, you will notice that nowhere in it does Wilber address the reality that a large percentage of the criticisms which he brushes off as being "first tier" are taking him to task for having *provably misrepresented* the purported "established facts" in the fields which he claims (falsely) to be integrating. Whether or not developmental studies are in "complete disarray," for example, Wilber has brutally misrepresented the purported agreement regarding Piaget's stages of psychological development. There is no way around that fact; so, not surprisingly, all kw can do in response is to claim that he understands the relevant fields much better than his harshest critics do ... thus apparently licensing him to utterly/unprofessionally misrepresent the ideas in those same fields ... and thus actually showing, for anyone who wishes to see, that he either hasn't understood them or is deliberately and dishonestly misleading his readers.

> I am not going to keep responding to the lunatics, nuts, fakes, and frauds.

But, into which group does the present author fit? Lunatic, nut, fake, or (well-footnoted) fraud? Or maybe a "perv" (Wilber's word) instead? (Yet, both Huston Smith and James Fadiman endorsed my since-disowned first book on Eastern philosophy with far greater enthusiasm than they have ever given publicly to any of Wilber's own attempts at scholarship. That, after all, is one good reason why he cannot openly include me in the "first-tier" category of those who purportedly cannot, even in principle, understand his ideas.)

From the same blog entry, this is a partial list of Wilber's fertile imaginings regarding the purported shortcomings of persons such as myself, who dare not only to have no use for his philosophy but to further point out, in reasoned detail, why his conjectures make so very little sense:

> lunatic and cacophonous ... so deranged as to be laughable ... suck my dick ... level of scholarship is so mediocre ... worthless ... you morons ... lame criticism ... painfully sluggish critics, dragging their bloated bellies across the ground at a snail's pace of gray dreariness, can frankly just eat my dust and bite my ass ... nonsensical ... neither true nor false but empty ... criticism so deranged you just stare at it wide-eyed and dumbfounded ... criticism so absolutely loopy you just stare in disbelief for minutes, pie-eyed, slack-jawed, say whaaaaaat? ... numb-nut young Turks and no-nut old Turks, many of whom have studied [my] work for up to 3 full hours....

As a wise man noted, all that one would have to do is read that blog by Wilber (and nothing else) to see why he is losing respect even from those academics who used to think he deserved his high standing in the transpersonal/integral community. Indeed, kw's childish response *makes him look much worse, in his character, than any criticism of him by others could ever have done.*

Regardless, if you have to "rape and pillage" the details in any field in order to get them to "fit" with your grand theorizings—as Wilber has done throughout his entire career, and without which intellectual abuse there would not be any AQAL or the like—*you are not integrating anything.* Conversely, when people see details to which you (kw) are "legally blind," and correspondingly reject your supposed "integrations," it is not because they are seeing *less* than you are, but rather because they are seeing *more.*

Ironic, to be sure. But the reality is that if you simply pay proper attention to details and to elementary research, you cannot be "integral," by Wilber's use of the term. Because it is exactly that attention to detail and broad knowledge-base which proves that things do not fit together—and most probably never will—in anything resembling the fashion which kw pretends they do. And then, because you will not accept his detail-ignoring claims, you can only be "first tier."

> The whole kit and caboodle of recent criticism just reeks of Nietzschean *resentiment* [*sic*]—in plain English, resentment, deep and long and ugly resentment (Wilber, 2006).

KW is royally fooling himself if he imagines that any of the recent criticisms by myself or Meyerhoff, for example, are based in envy, lack of "second-tier" perspective, or resentment deriving from his (ill-gotten) "success." Anyone who wants to deceive others by presenting fairy-tale ideas which have no real hope of being true is indeed on a well-traveled road to "success" in this world. But there are still those of us who would rather get our recognition the honest way.

If you are even a competent undergraduate student with a conscience, there is next to nothing for you to envy in Ken Wilber's work or character: you already have more of what makes a decent human being in you than kw will ever even want to recover from his own wasted life. All you can really learn from the likes of him is what *not* to do with your life, and how *not* to behave in attempting to make a name for yourself.

On June 11 of 2006, Wilber published a "Part II" to his previous diatribe, claiming to have only posted the earlier scolding as a "test."

First, from one of his fans, as quoted in that follow-up (2006a) piece:

> NEVER in over two years have I witnessed anything like this. THIS IS NOT WHAT YOU [KW] ARE REALLY LIKE. I repeat, I have NEVER seen you act like this.

Bauwens and Dallman, however, long ago saw that side of kw. He has shown enough of it in his mistreatment of the late David Bohm, too, the latter of which is in black and white by his own hand, as noted in the appendix to this book.

From another quoted Fan of Ken:

> Sometimes the most compassionate thing one can do is to cut down dangerous and terrorist egos.

Is that what we are now to Wilber's loyal followers? Dangerous "terrorist" egos? Being cut down "compassionately"? For trying to warn people that Wilber's teachings and community are not what they appear to be?

Another Fan:

> I read Meyerhoff's MS a couple of years ago. There were some interesting points here and there, but even these I assumed you would be capable of rebutting with little problem.

Why would Wilber's admirers assume that? On what possible grounds? And why would kw publish this excerpt, when it really only shows how little actual questioning his friends and followers are capable of?

In the same letter, Wilber and his quoted friends touched on the "big picture" nature of their ideas; the need to deeply understand integral notions before criticizing them; and the supposed responsibility of critics to provide reasonable alternatives to the ideas they are critiquing. They also suggested that anyone, particularly business executives and politicians, would first do an appropriate level of "due diligence" before becoming involved with the integral ideology.

First, note that details are not mere "gotchas," nor does taking a "50,000-foot view" release you from the obligation of squaring your overarching principles with an honest representation of each and every detail. It was exactly because of the confirmation (to within experimental accuracy) of the predictions of Einstein's theories that he and his ideas became famous. Without that precise validation, no one would even know his name today, much less care about the elegance of the core ideas underlying those theories. In the integral world, by contrast, you can trip over details, and even actively misrepresent them, as much as you like, and the followers in that field will only defend your reasons for doing so, rather than taking you to task for that gross unprofessionalism.

Further, when one can prove that the principles on which a theory is founded are false (or grossly misrepresented), one actually doesn't need to separately debunk its conclusions. If the premises are wrong, the conclusions will be wrong, too. (Of course, by pure chance, someone like Wilber may still manage to get a few conclusions right—as even Velikovsky did, in astronomy.)

In any case, in fields of real scholarship there has always been room for persons who merely gave harsh criticisms of the prevailing ideas, even without being able to offer better alternatives themselves. Never mind that, in the integral world, having an alternative will only be held against you, via the claim that in tearing kw's ideas down you are just trying to get your own work noticed.

Meyerhoff has done an appropriate level of due diligence, in going back to the original sources which Wilber claims support his view, to prove that they regularly do not. How has he been treated by the integral community for doing so? And, how many people who get interested in kw's ideas would even be able to find the time, much less the interest, to do the same? Without that, all they can do is trust that the community wouldn't let incompetent or dishonest work rise to the top. That trust, as we have seen, is *very* misplaced.

As to the politicians in the UN, or our world's corporate executives, as targets for integral proselytizing: They would not do even one-tenth of that work. Rather, they will just look at the roster of "big names" endorsing the fallacious integral ideas, and then proceed in the confidence that "a hundred thousand Wilber fans can't be wrong." Those are people, after all, who cannot look past an executive summary to the details in the first place.

Wilber himself:

> I got several calls from spiritual teachers around the country, and they all said almost exactly the same thing: "I wish I had the nerve to do this." That was a very common response, and many teachers went on to lament the "green swamp" their own *sanghas* [i.e., spiritual communities] seemed to be, "and what can I do about it?"

Yes, the "green swamp," after all, wants democracy and dialog in what is inherently a dictatorship. "What can I do about it?" Indeed: Any guru would like nothing better than to suppress that disrespectful talking-back.

KW again:

> you don't like us, you hate us, you hate I-I, you hate wilber, you hate this and you hate that—we heard you loud and clear. And we saw you. And now we know each other, don't we? **But was that you or your shadow responding?**

Personally, until around half a dozen years ago I was still considering donating money to the Integral Institute; it was only in documenting Wilber's provable and gross misrepresentations of David Bohm's work that I began to sour on him, and since then to find his life's work throughout exhibiting exactly the same dismal caliber of thought and research. If you can look at that simple following-of-the-evidence and see only projection or hatred ... well, as Wilber says, "What We Are, That We See."

More from a couple of Ken's admirers, in support of his "compassionate rage":

> I trust the meta-vision you see of human and social evolution, and if this posting as is serves the Kosmos, then so be it.

> I couldn't list all your third-tier reasons for this, but I deeply know that Integral resonates with, and works for, those who are ready for it. It is a truth that doesn't need a prop to stand.

Of course Wilber must be "third tier," uniquely able to judge the effect of his actions on the Kosmos. That should have been obvious by now. After all, the first thing any spiritual leader must learn is that you must always keep at least one step (in purported spiritual evolution) ahead of the followers. But, when a pandit/guru tries to tell you that you are "first tier" and shadow-projecting simply because you won't stand for being manipulated or misled, or that "second tier would get it, and that is who it was meant for"—well, "Fool me once, shame on you; fool me twice, shame on me."

Another Fan:

> Yes I was pissed off about [Integral University] hosts being referred to as minions ... fuck the crazy critic.

First "terrorist egos," and now "crazy," too. Would the most committed members of any cult behave any differently?

Personally, I had never publicly referred to Wilber's close followers as "minions." But, truth be told, that is exactly what I regard them as being. Their thoughts as included on the "I was only kidding" blog by kw have only confirmed that for me.

Yet another admirer of Ken:

[D]oes telling a group of mental masturbators that they're off the mark actually legitimize them in a way? If their intent is simply (!) to fantasize, they are unlikely to have the decency to be embarrassed at being caught once again with their pants down around their knees.

First, does the integral community not realize that they are seen by skeptics as being every bit as "crazy," and unworthy of legitimization, as they now view Wilber's critics? No, of course they don't realize that. But it is nevertheless true.

And how ironic, that they reduce cogent criticism to the status of fantasy, while elevating their own transpersonal fairy tales and outright delusions to the status of "reality." Myself, Meyerhoff, and other solid critics have nothing to be "embarrassed" about, if the previous lacking-in-substance blog entry by kw is the best that he can offer in terms of trying to prove us to be "mental masturbators."

And where is Wilber's own "decency"? Or his sense of embarrassment *at having been caught, repeatedly, with his own "pants down," blatantly and unconscionably fabricating information?* Or his understanding of humor, or of group dynamics/laughter, for that matter?

The best response actually came from Wilber's close friend, Stuart Davis:

it's fantastic, it's overdue, and i feel it is appropriate and proportionate in tone and content. i laughed out loud half a dozen times, and it's right on the money. how fucking LONG are you supposed to sit back without comment while these toxic, petty fuckers make preposterous attacks on work that's ten years old? and only one in a hundred even knows what the fuck they're talking about, because like it or not YOU'RE RIGHT TO SAY it is a cross-altitude issue. these green shits take pot shots at 2nd tier morning, noon, and night, and they are literally not capable of registering the content, the locations, the addresses, the altitude of 2nd tier. it's insane, and i'm relieved to see you calling a spade a spade in this way.

Speaking of psychological shadows, Davis could hardly be showing his own more clearly.

Still, all that he and Wilber's other anonymously quoted supporters are really doing, throughout the above, is to parrot what
Ken has previously told them about the "first-tier, green, wanna-
be," etc., nature of his critics. And in doing so, they are acting as
very effective mouthpieces for kw, to voice on his behalf what he
himself could not say without completely blowing his reputation as
a "compassionate, spiritually evolved scholar."

In any case, even work a decade old is certainly worth debunking, particularly for how the provable dishonesties and/or incompetencies in it reflect on the character of its author; and also, for how
the same shortcomings suggest the (un)likelihood that his current
work will stand up to future criticism. (See Smith, 2003; 2006; and
2006a.) Not to mention that, as others have noted, if Wilber-5
"transcends and includes" the decade-old Wilber-4, the debunking
of the latter will still be directly relevant even to kw's current
ideas.

The point of putting these criticisms of Wilber's work into
print is to do what one can to prevent others, not merely from
wasting their time on Wilber's fabrications, and not merely from
meditating to the point of developing clinical psychoses when they
think they are working toward psychological stage-growth. For, as
if those issues were not enough, with Wilber's continuing endorsements of various "problematic" gurus, surely more than one person
has already thrown his/her life away on exactly those "Great Realizers." If one were working *for* the integral movement, attempting
to stop such dangerous foolishness would rightly be called "com-
passion." Here, however, it gets you branded as a "petty fucker."

Davis himself, as per his "Universe Communion" song from
the *Self-Untitled* album, genuinely believes that the "Dagon" (*sic*)
tribal people received their purported knowledge of astronomy
from extraterrestrials. He actually says (1998) that the song was
"inspired by John E. Mack's wonderful book *Abduction,* which I
recommend to anyone open to new possibilities of what we perceive
as reality."

The late Dr. Mack was, of course, Harvard University's embarrassingly credulous "UFO expert" (Carroll, 2004).

And Wilber proudly puts all of the above pandering into (online) print, without so much as a twinge of realization as to how it
looks to the real world.

KW again:

I should mention that when IU opens we will be having specific classes, for those who want, where we analyze various
forum responses for their altitude, their levels and lines, and
their shadow elements.

Yes, nothing bonds an in-group like laughing together at the
flaws of their out-group critics, who just cannot see things as clearly as they, the "special ones," do. And that will be done at a "university," no less.

Another Fan of Ken:

all we have to do now is send people to that [initial, "Wyatt
Earpy"] blog and watch their response. if it freaks them out,
it's unlikely they would do very well in any type of second-
tier work. so at least we know. the thing is, K loves these
people, I've seen him work with them because he'll work with
anybody.

Yes, so will every guru-figure who has ever been caught in a
web of deceits, and been publicly exposed for it. They all still "love"
you, and would like nothing more than to see you cave to their
terms, so they can "work with" you at making you a better person.
That is, at teaching you how to progress spiritually by becoming
"more like them." (Also, note that the all-lower-case writing style of
these supporters of Wilber exactly mirrors his own use of that af-
fectation. It would be interesting to know how many of them wrote
in that way prior to becoming part of kw's inner circle, would it
not?)

And through all of that, has Wilber offered any cogent, intelligent response to any of his recent critics ... never mind to David
Lane's critique from 1996? No, of course not. What he has posted
could rather just as well have all been a deliberate smoke screen,
to distract from the real issue. That is, to obscure the fact that his
ideas consistently do not stand up to any kind of thorough questioning—a point which is hardly mitigated by him trotting out a
few anonymous "experts" who naïvely imagine the contrary.

Frank Visser—author of *Ken Wilber: Thought As Passion*
(with a foreword by kw) and at one time, with Michel Bauwens, a
founding member of the Integral Institute—gave his own (2006)
response to Wilber's bloggings:

Wilber writes: "Have you noticed that the people who com-
plain the most about the concept of boomeritis almost always
have the worst cases of it?" So what about the #1 crusader
against boomeritis himself? Looks like he has a particularly
bad case of it. Even jokingly mentioning "I am at the center
of the vanguard of the greatest social transformation in the
history of humankind" is telling. Sure, it's a joke. Or is it?
Why mention?....

I will not get caught in this game of praise and condem-
nation, so reminiscent of cultic milieus I have been in before.
Instead, I will tirelessly go on publishing writings which I
consider helpful in understanding integral philosophy. I may
be wrong, I may be right—but that's not the issue. [T]he issue is that there should be an open, public forum where all
voices can be heard. That's why Integral World is valuable.

Bauwens, too, posted several excellent responses to Wilber's
"integral meltdown." From "On the Logic of Cultism at the Integral
Institutes" (2006):

Being integral is increasingly being defined as: "agreeing
with Ken Wilber." This is the only critique being accepted
within the movement. And basically it takes the form of: yes
you are a genius, but wouldn't you consider that xxx. Such a
form of self-denigrating critique is the only one acceptable,
and it can only serve to strengthen the edifice and the influence of the master....

[Even without Joe Firmage's money in the founding of I-
I, and Don Beck's reinforcement of kw's narcissism] the total-
izing edifice and the particular personality of Wilber would
in all likel[i]hood have evolved in this way eventually....

Can there be any hope for such a movement? In my
opinion: none whatsoever. The point of no-return has long
passed.

And, from "Ken Wilber is Losing It" (2006a):

[Wilber's rant and *Boomeritis,* plus, I would add, kw's tele-
phone interviews as featured on Integral Naked] sounds like
the expression of a man desperately in need of confirmation
by the young, attempting to be "cool," but not quite knowing
how to do it, and revealing his own immaturity in the process....

At one point in our lives, we may seek a system of systems that may put to rest of fears of paradoxes and contradictions, showing how different truth claims can nevertheless be all true at some higher level of integration. But at another point in your life, if you are not intellectually and spiritually lazy, you have to learn again to live with the uncertainty of knowledge, and then, frankly, any reliance of a total edifice a la Wilber becomes counterproductive.

Personally, I agree strongly with nearly all of the points made in both of those fine postings.

Visser then published a truly excellent "companion article" to his own response to kw. From Chamberlain's (2006a) "Sorry, It's Just Over Your Head":

> I read many responses to Wilber's part I, and the only person who speaks as if he might actually feel anything remotely like actual "hate" toward Wilber is Geoffrey Falk, and I think that calling Falk "hateful" would require us to read more into Falk's way of expressing himself than may be there. But let's say for sake of argument that Falk hates Wilber and I-I.

I cannot quarrel with any of that. But, of course, we should always leave open the possibility that I, too, have been deliberately trying to "push the buttons" of Ken and his followers. You know, in addition to obviously enjoying saucily "calling a spade a spade" when it comes to leaders and followers with whom one sadly cannot reason. So, one might as well (generally justifiably) insult them (after having first proved them to be in the wrong) and hope that something gets through in all that.

Still, love or hate the way in which I express myself, it makes no difference to the validity of the criticisms I have made of kw's ideas (and character). And really, without those solid critiques, which the members of the integral world cannot counter even were they disposed to responding cogently rather than reflexively, would Wilber have been pushed to his embarrassing meltdown, with that being *very damaging* to I-I's grandiose "mission" in the world? Perhaps ... but perhaps not.

(I don't want to take too much "credit," since Meyerhoff's outstanding work seems to be bothering kw much more than mine, at least by name. Probably a significant part of the reason for that, though, is that my own previous work has again been endorsed by the respected likes of David Lane, John Horgan, Len Oakes and Susan Blackmore—not to mention Smith and Fadiman—whom Wilber cannot easily dismiss without undercutting his own high position in the world.)

It is an open question as to whether or not I personally "hate the sinner" in any of my irreverent ("Eighth Deadly Sin") criticisms of our world's gurus and pandits. But I certainly "hate the sin," no question about that! Anyone who tells me half-truths or worse to try to get me to cave to his ideas, in religion or otherwise, has picked the wrong person to try to deceive.

During the same period of these responses to Wilber's "Wyatt Earpy" postings, an anonymous blogger gave a fantastic analysis (reprinted in [Chamberlain, 2006a]) of kw's guru-like "card-playing"—in his claims that his behavior constituted a skillful teaching, that people failed to see that only for not having evolved to his high level, and that the objections to that "teaching" were based simply on his critics' psychological projections:

> Folks, outlining how and why this is classic cultic behavior is too elementary to even go into. Just pick up any book on the subject, or go read about the true root of all this: Adi Da....
>
> In the end, Ken is trying to silence critics/outsiders by asking that they simply STOP, which is all he really wants at this point. He asks that they take a moratorium on judging others, on loathing and condemning him. Notice that none of this addresses anything of any real substance; it's just an attempt to bring it to an end, with him still on top as the teacher. He is the game-master, after all. In real academic and/or spiritual circles (or within an adult community) such cards are considered completely and totally out of bounds. They only work in guru and cultic environments. Ken, PLEASE, you are the one who needs to STOP.
>
> Is there anyone at I-I with the courage to tell him this?....
>
> The herd mentality that Wilber should concern himself with is the herd mentality he encourages in his young followers, the groupthink, the in-group versus out-group dynamic, the loading of the language with jargon and psychobabble, the arrogance, narcissism, and grandiosity.

Is it not amazing that all of that cultic behavior has become so clear, through kw's own actions, that only people in complete denial (of which there are, sadly, plenty) could fail to see it?

More from Wilber (2006b):

> I want to be hated for the real me! I am perfectly capable of generating massive irritation all by myself—I don't need your shadow to do it. So please do me the honor of hating the real me!

Yes, that is precisely what I have been doing, though the "hating" thing is still an open question.

> Okay, jokes aside: Let's forgive and forget the past, and start afresh. And let's see who honestly wishes to deal with this, and who wants to continue gun-fighting their own shadows....
>
> Both sides could use a little confession, repentance, and forgiveness. I can say that, right here and now, I fully forgive any and all hurt that has been inflicted on me by **unfair and unwarranted accusations, criticisms, and condemnations**. With full heart, I sincerely mean that.

Yes, the magnanimous Wilber "forgives" his critics. Particularly the ones whose criticism is clearly warranted and inarguably valid, but which he can only deal with by absurdly pretending that he is being misunderstood by first-tier "morons" who have treated him unfairly.

How unbelievably self-centered of the man—to offer such "forgiveness" to others *without asking, nay begging, for the same from them.*

Wikipedia (2006b), then, has this to say on the subject of narcissism:

> While in regression, the person displays childish, immature behaviors. He feels that he is omnipotent, and misjudges his power and that of his opposition. He underestimates challenges facing him and pretends to be "Mr. Know-All." His sensitivity to the needs and emotions of others and his ability to empathize with them deteriorate sharply. He becomes intolerably haughty and arrogant, with sadistic and paranoid tendencies. Above all, he then seeks unconditional admiration, even when others with more objective views per-

ceive that he does not deserve it. He is preoccupied with fantastic, magical thinking and daydreams. In this mode he tends to exploit others, to envy them, and to be explosive.

That, of course, matches Wilber's behaviors point-by-point. From his childish bloggings, to his misjudging of his most cogent critics as "morons" compared to his own "brilliance," to his know-it-all nature, to his insensitive "forgiving" of others (and simultaneous failure to ask for forgiveness himself) when he is clearly the one in the wrong. And more, to his haughtiness and arrogance, to his paranoid (i.e., disproportionate to reality) feelings of being loathed and condemned, to his obvious need for undeserved unconditional admiration. And from there to his certainty, from his own misinterpreted experiences, that paranormal phenomena and mystical winds exist—implying the magical ability of *his* thoughts to influence the world around him. And finally to his unconscionable manipulation and exploitation of others to ensure his own "greatness."

Completely consistent with that diagnosis, Matthew Dallman (2005a) has independently noted, of Wilber:

> I have ... never met a more self-absorbed person....
>
> Any real teacher is someone abundant in their help; in my experience, and according to accounts of several long-time associates, Wilber helps no one unless it serves to help him and his reputation....
>
> It also turned out that what I thought was a think-tank [i.e., the Integral Institute] was, in reality, a company, which went on to produce products like any company would. Those products include self-help DVDs, for-pay websites promising exclusive access to him, as well as expensive seminars and experiential workshops. Essentially, the whole thing is to sell Wilber as well as his model, even if advertised otherwise.

And to what may kw look forward, in his own "psychological development"?

> A personality disorder arises only when repeated attacks on the obstacle continue to fail—especially if this recurrent failure happens during the formative stages (0–6 years of age). The contrast between the fantastic world (temporarily) occupied by the individual and the real world in which he keeps being frustrated (the grandiosity gap) is too acute to counte-

nance for long. The dissonance gives rise to the unconscious "decision" to go on living in the world of fantasy, grandiosity and entitlement (Wikipedia, 2006b).

Of course, Wilber is blessed to not have to retreat into complete fantasy in order to live all that out: He has already created the "reality" of the Integral Institute in which to act out his delusions of greatness and entitlement.

Len Oakes wrote an entire book (*Prophetic Charisma*) on the typically narcissistic personality structure of cult leaders. What we are seeing with kw is just par for the course and would, as Bauwens has noted, have happened eventually even without any "critical" provocation: Wilber was always an "institute" waiting to happen.

On June 22, 2006, in the third installment of his "Wyatt Earp" series of blog postings, Wilber (2006c) gave his best yet still embarrassingly limping arguments, as to why his Integral Institute is supposedly not a cult:

> Based on a year-long study ... we arrived at this 3-variable, 8-box grid, which has continued to be highly accurate in spotting and predicting cultic behavior, because it is based, not on making judgments like "it doesn't allow criticism" (which is meaningless), but rather on several nonjudgmental variables that have been found empirically to be associated with behavior that injures groups and individuals. (This stops people who don't like a movement from labeling it cultic by coming up with checklists of things they don't like, which are just tautological.) It was, and is indeed, a landmark publication.
>
> [Actually, a lot has happened over the past twenty years in the cult-studies field and elsewhere; what was (wrongly) regarded as being insightful back then, hasn't necessarily stood the test of time. Who in the cult-studies field actually uses the ideas in kw's co-written *Spiritual Choices* today? No one that I am aware of; I cannot recall even having seen the book cited, and have read it only because it is part of kw's "canon" of supposedly "landmark" works.]
>
> I am glad to report that both the structure and beliefs of Integral Institute fall in the box (out of 8 boxes) that, in the past, has had the lowest number of cultic behaviors.... There are all sorts of other integral philosophies, integral forums, and arenas where somebody can play if they reject our ap-

proach, and I support the existence of those other forums and always have.

Yes, you are welcome to go and "play," as children do, with some other guru or organization if you cannot take the heat at I-I, or if you are simply too unevolved to understand the Great Work they imagine themselves to be doing. "So long, Failure. You never even existed here." Ask Matthew Dallman (2005a): "I was the first composer featured on that site, but any reference to me was removed after I resigned from IU." Plus, kw's previously reported regard for "arenas" such as the California Institute of Integral Studies as being "cesspools" can hardly be reconciled with his more recent, strategic equanimity.

In any case, I already have a whole chapter in *Stripping the Gurus* pointedly titled "Spiritual Choices," debunking the false claims to excellence of Wilber's book of the same name. Have the "8 boxes" of kw and his co-authors really "continued to be highly accurate in spotting and predicting cultic behavior"? No, they have not. From STG, as published well over a year prior to Wilber's self-endorsement of *Spiritual Choices:*

> Incredibly, most of the "enlightened" individuals and ashrams included herein would have been considered to fall close to the "safest" of the categories in the typologies of Dick Anthony (1987), et al., via the *Spiritual Choices* book. That is, nearly all of the spiritual teachers we have met thus far (not including the leaders of the Hare Krishnas, Moonies, or Jim Jones) were:
>
> - Monistic rather than dualistic—i.e., working toward realizing a state of inherent conscious oneness with all things, as opposed to placing God as inexorably separate from creation and approachable only through a unique savior such as Jesus, with the failure to follow the appropriate savior leading to eternal damnation (exceptions: none)
>
> - Multilevel—i.e., having a "distinct hierarchy of spiritual authority," in gnosis versus teachings versus interpretations (unilevel exceptions, which "confuse real and pseudo-transcendence of mundane consciousness," include Findhorn, Scientology, Rajneesh and Transcendental Medita-

tion® [notwithstanding that the Maharishi's teachings themselves are rooted in the Vedas]), and

- Non-charismatic—i.e., emphasizing techniques of spiritual transformation (e.g., meditation), rather than relying on a personal relationship between disciple and teacher as the means of evolution/enlightenment of the former (exceptions: Ramakrishna, Meher Baba, Neem Karoli Baba, Adi Da, Muktananda, Ma Jaya Sati Bhagavati, Jetsunma, Cohen, and Sai Baba and Chinmoy to lesser degrees)

Chögyam Trungpa, Swami Satchidananda and Zen Buddhism were all explicitly placed in Anthony's "safest" category—of "multilevel, technical monism." In his second-safest grouping ("multilevel, charismatic monism") we find Meher Baba, Neem Karoli Baba, Muktananda, Chinmoy and Adi Da.

If those are "safe" spiritual leaders and communities, though, one shudders to think what "dangerous" ones might look like. One's jaw drops further to find that, as late as 2003, Wilber has still been recommending *Spiritual Choices* to others as a means of distinguishing "safe" groups from potentially "problematic" ones. That such recommendations are coming years after the central thesis (as documented above) of the text has been wholly discredited in practice, is astounding.

Fooled by the arguments of Anthony, et al., I myself had endorsed *Spiritual Choices* at one point in a previous work. Obviously, however, my opinion of that book and of its authors' ideas has matured significantly since then. Indeed, by this point I very much regret that previous naïvete on my part, particularly when it is coupled with ideas such as the following, from the same group of "experts":

[Tom] Robbins and [Dick] Anthony's own contribution [to *In Gods We Trust* (1982)] includes a superb introduction—perhaps the best single chapter in the anthology; a complete and devastating critique of the brainwashing model; and an insightful report on the Meher Baba community (Wilber, 1983b).

The relevant meager, twelve-page, utterly simplistic chapter on brainwashing, however, is anything but a "complete" critique, much less a "devastating" one. Whatever one may think of the brainwashing and mind-control debate, how could a five-thousand word treatment of that complex subject possibly be "complete"? Entire books have been written from both sides of the controversy without exhausting it; entire Library of Congress Cataloguing in Publication designations exist for the subject! Even if the short paper in question were the greatest ever written, *it could not possibly be "complete"!*

For myself, I have found the chapter in question to be utterly unimpressive. Indeed, it shows near-zero understanding of the psychological factors influencing one's "voluntary joining," and later difficulty in leaving, such environments. There is nothing whatsoever "devastating" about the text, whether one agrees or disagrees with Anthony's overall perspective....

For a revealing example of Anthony's own wilber-esque attempts at critiquing other scholars' ideas, see Zablocki (2001).

Further, it is well-known that destructive cults also form around political and psychological leaders. In those cases, the "important" dichotomies of monistic vs. dualistic, and of multilevel vs. unilevel, are completely absent. That is, Wilber and Anthony's "matrix" reduces to simply whether the group follows techniques of (political?) transformation, or relies on a personal relationship between follower and leader! So, in any non-spiritual context, their "landmark" contributions there reduce to merely *two boxes.* One could hardly do better for exhibiting binary, black-or-white thinking.

Thus, even if the matrix worked in terms of reliably evaluating spiritual communities, it would be all-but-useless in any of the other contexts in which one needs to evaluate whether or not a given group is a destructive cult. That should be a glaring indication that the criteria given by Wilber and Anthony for spotting potentially destructive spiritual groups have little relevance indeed to reality.

Plus, in terms of tautologies, we have Wilber using his own past theorizings to "prove" that his current community is okay. But those previous theorizings (by himself and the utterly misled "cult-apologist" Dick Anthony [see Ross, 2003]) were, of course, created from within exactly the same psychological blinders which have produced his current community.

*If* "it doesn't allow criticism" is a meaningless criterion for defining what a cult is, then how about "it doesn't allow persons to make competent, thorough and valid criticisms of its leaders' teachings or character, which the leaders cannot refute, while still permitting the questioners to remain members in good standing of the community"? That, at any rate, is exactly how one could reasonably describe Wilber's institute and surroundings.

KW again:

> Ordinarily you would tell somebody that their capacity to love is wonderful, something to be nurtured and increased. The more they love, the better. EXCEPT if they love me. If they feel any sort of love for me and say so, then they are a cultic idiot. So apparently if anybody loves me, they are sick.

If, after becoming aware of Meyerhoff's and my own work (etc.) in exposing Wilber for the manipulative spiritual leader that he is, you *still don't get what kw is up to,* well, then yes, I cannot see any other conclusion than that there must be powerful factors in your own psychology blinding you to that reality. And those are indeed some of the same factors which get people into, and life-long stuck in, even the worst recognized cults.

And if, after having had it demonstrated to you that a person's "philosophy" cannot manage to be self-consistent even in the midst of its gross and inexcusable violations of truth, you still continue to accept that worldview as being valid ... well, in any non-spiritual field of knowledge you certainly would not be regarded as thinking clearly or competently.

Nevertheless, those of us who have been through cults ourselves don't generally refer to other people, who in the absence of proper debunking of their leaders may simply be as gullible as we once were, as being "cultic idiots." (In the cult-studies field, with its emphasis on coercive persuasive, a.k.a. "brainwashing," they would *never* refer to followers in that way.) I have indeed used the phrase "integral idiots" to describe followers of Wilber who go out intent on teaching (or censoring) me, for example, without having first done their homework; I have even referred to the same people as "dumb FOKs" (Fans of Ken). But that is very different from viewing anyone as being a "cultic idiot" simply for "loving" Wilber.

If you can love a raging narcissist, who by all believable reports will "love" you back only so long as you are useful to him,
more power to you. But even then, don't get fooled by his "theories," because as soon as you go back to primary sources to verify
their supporting claims, it all falls apart, and the manipulations of
their author become obvious for anyone with eyes to see.

Far too many of the individuals fawningly expressing their
"love" for kw in the wake of his "Wyatt Earpy" bloggings were, I
think, not merely "loving the sinner" but also "loving the sin." That
is, lapping up the clear manipulation in which Wilber was overtly
indulging, and correspondingly being utterly unwilling or unable to
evaluate that critically and see it for what it really is.

As anyone familiar with Wilber's work knows, the *context* in
which such needy "love" is expressed matters immensely; kw "skillfully" omits that fact from his above "analysis." The problem is not
that his followers "love" him and openly express that sentiment in
spite of his glaring character flaws and the near-worthlessness of
his "theories." Rather, the worrisome thing is how they feel the
need to gushingly express how they were moved to tears by his
great and "compassionate" teaching methods in the very midst of
being blatantly manipulated, with that unsettling reaction being
presented as proof of their own "second-tier," "saved" status in the
unquestioning community. And yes, when "love" is expressed in
that context it is indeed disturbingly cultic.

All of that is a far cry from Wilber's simplistic, sadly controlling and narcissistically paranoid framing of the issue as being "if
anybody loves me, they are sick." But then, kw didn't get to where
he is today by paying attention to nuances.

> [Wilber] may have footnotes galore, but he is no scholar. He
> is a speculator who co-opts the insights of others.... He is the
> parasite, not his critics, and not the thinkers/scholars whose
> shoulders he wants to stand on. As demonstrated by this
> ["Wyatt Earpy"] "essay," this man's ideas are sick, his inten-
> tions laughably irrelevant. Seeing some of his endorsed de-
> fenders in their ghastly display of non-thinking, it is clear
> that he infects the thoughts and words of others like a virus
> ... baldly embodying all that he criticizes in others (Dallman,
> 2006).

Sad, but very true. Or, as Meyerhoff (2006c) noted:

The way I see it, my critique and that of others has left so little of Wilber's integral synthesis standing that he has to devise ways to avoid responding to them in order to fool his followers, and probably himself, into thinking that his system is the best integration of contemporary knowledge available. Wilber's techniques of avoidance are long and getting longer....

My conclusion is that the emperor has few clothes. The cowboy is circling the wagons to better defend an untenable position. He's been exposed and can't confront it nor admit it, and so he avoids critical engagement through an array of diversions.

But then, we could have anticipated no small part of all that simply from Wilber's longstanding, gross misrepresentations of the positions of even his mildest critics, in Rothberg and Kelly's aforementioned (1998) *Ken Wilber in Dialogue*.

First, Michael Washburn:

Wilber's exposition of my ideas in his response is marred by egregious misrepresentations....

Wilber formulates my view *backwards* ... [and] attributes his own metaphysical assumptions to me.

And then, Stanislav Grof:

[S]ome of the concepts or statements that Ken attributes to me and criticizes me for, have not been part of any stage of my intellectual evolution.

And finally, Peggy Wright:

I have found Wilber's presentation [in SES] in the area of human evolution and development to be at odds with a number of sources that are listed in his bibliography....

So, the pattern has always been there, in terms of Wilber's despicably unprofessional methods of responding to even his most overly respectful critics. It has been there, too, in his egregious misrepresentations of the ideas of his sources, being always twisted only as to support his own position.

# CHAPTER X

# THE STRANGE CASE
# OF KEN WILBER

Zen teachers have an excellent method of dealing with students who start comparing themselves to Buddha or God [after their early enlightenment experiences, says Ken Wilber]. "They take the stick and beat the crap out of you. And after five or ten years of that, you finally get over yourself" (Horgan, 2003a).

"Crazy wisdom" occurs in a very strict ethical atmosphere (Wilber, 1996).

NO PRESENTATION OF THE FOIBLES of Ken Wilber would be complete without a look at his endorsements of the "crazy wisdom" gurus Andrew Cohen and Adi Da, his associated praising of various forms of purportedly beneficial spiritual violence, and a further analysis of the predictable extensions of his own admitted psychological motivations to his own behaviors.

First, kw's writings have traditionally generated a uniquely high level of interest within the inner circle of Andrew Cohen's community. Andrew's now-former disciple Andre van der Braak had actually done his psychology thesis on Wilber, piquing Cohen's curiosity with his associated bookshelves full of kw's ponderous works, and resulting in their reported collective brainstorming as to how to get Wilber in as a student of Cohen's:

> We speculate about why he hasn't been willing to meet with Andrew. *Is he afraid of ego death?* (van der Braak, 2003; italics added).

Their persistent courting evidently paid off, however, for in Wilber's foreword to Cohen's (2002) *Living Enlightenment* we read:

> [Rude Boys] live as Compassion—real compassion, not idiot compassion—and real compassion uses a sword more often than a sweet. They deeply offend the ego (and the greater the offense, the bigger the ego)....
>
> Andrew Cohen is a Rude Boy. He is not here to offer comfort; he is here to tear you into approximately a thousand pieces ... so that Infinity can reassemble you....
>
> Every deeply enlightened teacher I have known has been a Rude Boy or Nasty Girl. The original Rude Boys were, of course, the great Zen masters, who, when faced with yet another ego claiming to want Enlightenment, would get a huge stick and whack the aspirant right between the eyes.... Rude Boys are on your case in the worst way, they breathe fire, eat hot coals, will roast your ass in a screaming second and fry your ego before you knew what hit it....
>
> I have often heard it said that Andrew is difficult, offending, edgy, and I think, "Thank God." In fact, virtually every criticism I have ever heard of Andrew is a variation on, "He's very rude, don't you think?"

However, Luna Tarlo's (1997) exposé of Cohen (*Mother of God*) had been published nearly *half a decade before* Wilber's penning of that odd mixture of images. (Tarlo is Cohen's Jewish mother, who has compared her son's promises of deliverance from suffering, through the use of his own power, to those of Hitler.) Had kw properly informed himself of that, he would most certainly have heard criticisms of Cohen which could *in no way* be dismissed as arising merely from overly sensitive egos complaining about not being sufficiently coddled. (Needless to say, Cohen disputes the accuracy of the depiction of life in his communities given by his own mother, and presumably does not agree with van der Braak's sketching of it, either. The WHAT enlightenment??! website [http://whatenlight enment.blogspot.com], though, offers many additional, generally equally uncomplimentary stories from other former disciples.)

If being a "Rude Boy" simply means speaking unpleasant truths, then yes, "every deeply enlightened teacher" has probably done that. Such beneficial behavior, however, is *vastly* different from what Cohen is alleged to have indulged in.

Further, just because a "master" is a "Rude Boy" toward others *obviously does not mean* that his own "breakthrough" into claimed radical enlightenment was the product of having previously been treated in that way himself. Indeed, neither the late (d. 2008) Adi Da nor Cohen have recorded their own enlightenments as arising from being on the receiving end of such behavior. That fact is radically significant, as is the fact that neither Cohen nor Da, explicitly, have managed to produce *even one* disciple as "enlightened" as they themselves claim to be, in spite of their "rude" behaviors.

> It does have to be considered at this point that there are no practitioners in the advanced and ultimate stages (Da, in [Elias, 2000]).

> None of Cohen's students have become liberated (Horgan, 2003).

Beyond that, the whole disturbingly violent "whack between the eyes" thing is a rather absurdly romanticized view of Zen. Indeed, one cannot help but wonder: Has Wilber himself ever received such a beneficial, hard blow between the eyes with a huge stick, or literally had the crap beaten out of him? Was that what brought on any of his early, "verified" *satoris,* or his nondual One Taste realization? If not, he has no business recommending such treatment to others.

In addition to attempting to spread his teachings through his books and personal counsel within his spiritual community, in 1992 Cohen founded *What Is Enlightenment?* magazine. (He has also recently arranged to partner with The Graduate Institute in Connecticut, in an accredited program of studies: www.learn.edu/ wie.htm.) That periodical has been praised by Wilber (in Cohen, 2002) as follows:

Andrew's magazine ... is the only [one] I know that is ... asking the hard questions, slaughtering [needlessly violent macho imagery, again] the sacred cows, and dealing with the Truth no matter what the consequences.

Notably, the June/August 2006 issue of *What Is Enlightenment?* was largely devoted to the life's work of their "favorite integral prophet," Ken Wilber. (Yes, they explicitly called him a "prophet.")

Many years earlier, in 1980, Wilber had penned a foreword for Adi Da's *Scientific Proof of the Existence of God Will Soon Be Announced by the White House!* Most of it was spent in arguing that Da was not creating a harmful "cult" around himself, but Wilber also found space to include the following praise:

[M]y opinion is that we have, in the person of Da Free John, a Spiritual Master and religious genius of the ultimate degree. I assure you I do not mean that lightly. I am not tossing out high-powered phrases to "hype" the works of Da Free John. I am simply offering to you my own considered opinion: Da Free John's teaching is, I believe, unsurpassed by that of any other spiritual Hero, of any period, of any place, of any time, of any persuasion.

Not finished with hyperbole—or "syrupy devotionalism," as one critic (Kazlev, 2003) reasonably put it—in 1985 Wilber contributed effusive text for the front matter of Adi Da's *The Dawn Horse Testament:*

This is not merely my personal opinion; this is a perfectly obvious fact, available to anyone of intelligence, sensitivity, and integrity: *The Dawn Horse Testament* is the most ecstatic, most profound, most complete, most radical, and most comprehensive single spiritual text ever to be penned and confessed by the Human Transcendental Spirit.

Obviously, any sincere seeker reading such ecstatic praise from the most highly respected "genius" in consciousness studies might be inclined to experience for himself the teachings of such a unique, "greatest living" (Wilber's words) Adept. Indeed, had I come across those endorsements in my own (teenage years, at the time) search, and been aware of and unduly awed by Wilber's status in the consciousness-studies community, I myself might well

have foolishly taken such exaggerations seriously enough to experience Adi Da's community discipline first-hand.

How unsettling, then, to discover a 1987 interview with *Yoga
Journal,* only a few short years after the *Dawn Horse* praises,
where Wilber stated his opinion that Adi Da's "entire situation has
become very problematic." Nearly a *decade* later (1996a), he explained: "'Problematic' was the euphemism that sociologists at that
time were using for Jonestown."

For my own part, not being a sociologist, I would never have
caught on to the meaning of that word without having it explained
to me ... albeit years after the fact, here. I suspect that I am not
alone in that regard.

No matter: Three years later, in 1990, Wilber was back to con-
tributing endorsements for Da's teachings, this time to the humbly
titled *The Divine Emergence of the World-Teacher:*

> The event of Heart-Master Da is an occasion for rejoicing,
> for, *without any doubt whatsoever,* he is the first Western
> Avatar to appear in the history of the world.... His Teaching
> contains the most concentrated wealth of transcendent wis-
> dom found anywhere, I believe, in the spiritual literature of
> the world, modern or ancient, Eastern or Western (in Bond-
> er, 1990; italics added).

Note that, in the above quote, Wilber is evidently considering
himself fit not merely to pronounce on the degree of enlightenment
of others, but even to confirm their avatar status, "without any
doubt whatsoever."

Of the above author Saniel Bonder (2003) himself—who has
since independently adopted the status of teacher, without Adi
Da's blessing—Wilber has more recently declared:

> Saniel Bonder is one in whom the Conscious Principle is
> awakened.

Again, note the oracular nature of the statement, as no mere
expression of opinion, but rather as a without-doubt, categorical
evaluation of another person's spiritual enlightenment—as if Wilber himself was able to see into others' minds, or clairvoyantly dis-
cern their degree of conscious evolution.

Others, however, have reasonably questioned the possibility,
even in principle, of anyone executing such radical insight:

[B]oth mystics and sympathetic writers about mysticism are just wrong if they think that there is a way of telling whether the other person has had a genuine experience or just pretends to have had one....

A man may write excellent love poetry without ever having been a comparable lover; it is the writer's skill as a writer that makes his words convincing, not his skill as a lover. The mystic's talk about his experience may be skillful or clumsy, but that does not improve or weaken his actual experience (Bharati, 1976).

Bharati himself was both a scholar and a swami of the Ramakrishna Order.

Seven years before the aforementioned "problematic" *Yoga Journal* piece, Wilber (in Da, 1980) had again ironically been "protesting too much," in print, that Adi Da was not creating a harmful environment around himself:

[N]owhere is [Da] more critical of the "cultic" attitude than he is towards those who surround him.... I have never heard Da Free John criticize anyone as forcefully as he does those who would approach him chronically from the childish stance of trying to win the favor of the "cultic hero."

Other fans of Da—even those who have comparably considered him to be "the ultimate expression of the Truth residing in all religions"—however, have claimed to find in his followers exactly what Wilber would evidently rather not see:

The problem was they were much too friendly, much too happy, and far too nice. More plainly put, they were all busy breathlessly following their own bliss. Not only this, but unless my eyes were deceiving me, *they all looked like maybe they came from the same neighborhood or the same college.* It was uncanny really. And very disquieting, as well. I mean, they all looked and sounded almost exactly alike.

My God, they're pod people, I thought (Thomas Alhburn, in [Austin, 1999]; italics added).

Hassan (1990) gives a completely plausible explanation for such phenomena:

One reason why a group of [alleged] cultists may strike even a naïve outsider as spooky or weird is that everyone has similar odd mannerisms, clothing styles, and modes of speech. What the outsider is seeing is the personality of the leader passed down through several layers of modeling.

Wilber closed his aforementioned (1996a) admonitions regarding Da—sequestered in Fiji, by that point—with the relative caution that, until the day when the "World Teacher consents to enter the World," one might just keep a "safe distance" as a student of Da's writings, rather than as a resident of his community. As to how Adi Da "re-entering the world" from his island seclusion would alleviate the "problematic" aspects of his teachings, however, that was not made clear.

By comparison, would Jim Jones re-entering the world from his isolated agricultural commune in Guyana have made *his* teachings safe? If not, why would a comparable re-entry have been the solution to the "problematic" (Wilber's word) aspects of Adi Da? Isn't it better for the world at large—if not for their unfortunate, already duped followers—if these individuals *do* isolate themselves?

At any rate, none of the above milquetoast caveats from Wilber have ever been included in any of his books, where they might have reached "a hundred thousand" people (Wilber, 2000a). Rather, in terms of kw's own attempts at promoting that version of reality, the (1996a) letter exists, at the time of this writing, only on his (publishers') website ... buried in the Archives section, not sharing the home page with his many accolades.

Wilber later (1998a) offered an explanatory open letter to the Adi Da community. That was posted *anonymously* (i.e., evidently not by Ken himself) on the Shambhala KW Forum for date 8/1/01 in the Open Discussion area, a full three years after the fact. (That forum itself has existed since early 2000.) There, he clarified his position on Da, back-tracking significantly from any insight which one might have been tempted to credit him from 1996, and explicitly stating that he had not renounced his view of (or love for, or devotion toward) Da as Realizer. Rather, he argued simply that Adi Da's "World Teacher" status enjoindered upon him the maintaining of a presence in the world, and the initiation of an "even more aggressive outreach program" by the community, as opposed to his ongoing seclusion.

An *"even more aggressive outreach program."* To put a positive spin on a "problematic" situation, and "spread the word" to more people, thereby doing *more* harm? Or perhaps simply to warn potential devotees as to what they're getting themselves into, as if that would then clear up all of the reported problems with the community?

As posters in Bob (2000)—themselves making no claim to genius, but clearly adept in common sense—have insightfully (and independently) pointed out:

> I find it absurd that Wilber seems to attach more importance to criticizing Da's failure to appear in public forums than he does to examining the very serious [alleged] abuses of trust and misuse of power that have [reportedly] been perpetrated by Da under the guise of spiritual teaching. In light of the well-documented [reported] problems that Da has created in his own life and his follower's [*sic*] lives, it is completely irrelevant to any evaluation of Da whether or not he accepts Ken's challenge to go out into the world at large. Who cares! Why would anyone want to see Da broaden his influence by speaking to a larger audience?

The full text of Wilber's aforementioned (1998a) open letter to the Daist Community is eminently worth reading, toward one's own disillusion regarding the caliber of advice given by even the "brightest lights" in the spiritual marketplace. To summarize its contents: Wilber states that he neither regrets nor retracts his past endorsements of Adi Da; that it is only for cultural and legal considerations that he can no longer publicly give a blanket recommendation for people to follow Da; that he is pleased that his own writings have brought people to Da Avatar and hopes that they will continue to have that effect in the future; and that he still recommends that "students who are ready" become disciples/devotees of Da.

A month and a half after distributing the above nuggets of wisdom to the Adi Da community, Wilber (1998b) reconfirmed his position in another open letter, posted as of this writing on his website. There, he states that the "real difficulty of 'the strange case of Adi Da' is that the guru principle *is neither understood nor accepted by our culture*" (italics added). He further opines (italics again added) that for those individuals who realize full well the extremely risky nature of the *adventure,* but who feel a strong pull toward *complete and total surrender* of their lives to a spiritual Master, I can certainly recommend Adi Da.... [H]e is one of the greatest spiritual Realizers of all time, in my opinion.

Note further that the related title, "The Strange Case of Franklin Jones," was used in 1996 by David Lane and Scott Lowe, in their exposés of Da/Jones and his ashram environment. Unless that was a common phrase going around in the mid-'90s, then, it would seem that Wilber was likely aware of their earlier, insightful critique of the dynamics reportedly going on within Adi Da's community. Rather than properly absorbing the information in that, however, he has evidently simply seen fit to give his own, purportedly more valuable version of the same—even though looking on merely from a safe distance, not as a first-hand, residential participant. That is sad, since Lowe and Lane have offered real insight into the situation, while Wilber has consistently failed miserably to do the same.

One further assumes that in praising Da's spiritual state, Wilber was referring more to the man's later realizations than to early insights such as the following:

I remember once for a period of days I was aware of a world that appeared to survive in our moon. It was a superphysical or astral world where beings were sent off to birth on the Earth or other worlds, and then their bodies were enjoyed cannibalistically by the older generation on the moon, or they were forced to work as physical and mental slaves (Da, 1995).

Of course, unless one is inclined to take the visions of "astral moon cannibal slaves" on the part of Da Guru seriously, one arrives at serious concerns as to Adi Da's mental stability. After all, skeptics have long rightly held that even a single instance of any given medium or sage being caught "cheating" in "manifesting" objects, casts doubt on every "miracle" that had previously been attributed to the individual. Likewise, if even one aspect of an individual's enlightenment has been hallucinated but taken as real, the potential exists for it to *all* have been the product of delusion in a psychiatric, not a metaphysical, sense.

So you have to ask yourself: Do *you* believe that there are B-movie-like "cannibal masters/slaves" on the astral counterpart to our moon?

Wilber, at least, seems (in Da, 1985) to have no doubt, overall:

> I am as certain of this Man as I am of anything I have written.

That statement may be more understandable if one considers the following:

> It is possible to look at [Wilber's] early but seminal book *The Atman Project* and see how his idea of successive stages of psycho-spiritual development grew out of Da's seven stages of life thesis (Kazlev, 2003).

The purported day-long manifestation by Da of a "corona" around the physical sun was included as a documented "miracle" in his (1974) self-published *Garbage and the Goddess*. Further, since Wilber had read that book prior to writing the above 1980 and 1985 forewords—it is listed in the bibliography for his (1977) *Spectrum of Consciousness*—one must ask: Does this mean that he was accepting that apparently non-existent "miracle" (which skeptics in the community did not see) as being valid? One cannot help but assume so, since the alternative would be to say that Wilber regarded Da as not accurately presenting his spiritual accomplishments, but still chose to pen his complimentary forewords.

In the face of such gushing as all the above, one begins to suspect that no small amount of the praise given to "greatest Realizers," etc., might likely derive from the related hope that, the more one celebrates one's own heroes, the more others may celebrate you as *their* hero in the same unquestioning and hyperbolic manner.

Wilber's posting of Brad Reynolds' (2004) comparing of him to the Buddhist god Manjushri, comparable to his own childish attitude with regard to Adi Da, certainly does nothing to dispel the above "tit for tat" suspicions: "See? *This* is how you should treat *me.*"

Or as Kate Strelley (1987) noted after having left Bhagwan Rajneesh's Poona ashram to be feted as a celebrity at a relatively minor center in England:

[W]hat I really got off on was the fact that *I* was now being
treated in the way I would treat Sheela.

One could substitute the name of any guru-figure or foolish
pandit for the one-time respected administrator Sheela in that,
and it would apply just as well.

Of course, in any such context, you could not then speak out
properly against even the radical shortcomings in your own one-
time heroes, as that would then license your followers to do the
same to you. That is, the only way to teach others how to treat you
with proper respect would be to continue to speak publicly with
exaggerated regard for the idols. That must continue even long after it was obvious that they were not what they claimed to be, and
even if one could, when pressed, admit to the latter when safe from
the public eye.

Thus:

> In private correspondence with me (and in person), Wilber
> has admitted that "Da is a fuck-up" (his words, not mine)
> (Lane, 1996).

Of course, it may also be that Wilber is simply so desperate for
his (now-late) hero Adi Da's approval, love and attention that he
will (publicly) do everything in his power to retain that. But that
would be even less flattering than the above explanation, as an explicitly immature, dependent stance.

Still, as Chögyam Trungpa's former disciple Stephen Butterfield (1994) noted:

> In the guru/disciple relationship, [the] self-conscious longing
> for acceptance, regarded as a form of devotion, operates to
> intimidate the student into deference.

And then, from the deferential Wilber (1998a):

> I affirm my own love and devotion to the living Sat-Guru
> [i.e., Adi Da].... I send ... a deep bow to Master Adi Da.

Wilber himself, interestingly, had elsewhere and earlier (in
Anthony, et al., 1987) mocked followers who view their spiritual
leader as being a "perfect master":

[H]ow great the guru is; in fact, how great I must be to be among the chosen. It is an extremely narcissistic position.

Indeed it is, particularly since the difference between "perfect master" and "greatest living Realizer" is hardly significant. That minimal difference, further, is essentially irrelevant in this context. For, one will again obviously feel extremely special for being noticed or chosen (e.g., to write forewords) by any "greatest" Realizer, even if the latter is not "perfect." "Extremely narcissistic" is thus absolutely right, but for the integral goose as well as for the gander. As Radzik (2005) noted:

People look to gurus as a way to get self acceptance. If they can get acceptance from the guru, then of course they must be okay. The more powerful and magical and mystical the guru is, the more valuable his/her acceptance is. Therefore, the tendency is to elevate the guru to superhuman mythical god-man status.

Another former follower of Da expressed his own perspective (in Bob, 2000) with comparable insight:

Hell, saying he's realized at all may be just a way to make myself seem less of a sucker for biting, and to avoid dissing people I respect who are still into him.

Notwithstanding all that, as late as 1998 Wilber was again still publicly defending Adi Da, even after having reportedly given the more negative evaluations in private at least two years earlier. Most likely, what he then means is that Da is a "fuck-up" along moral lines or the like, but is still the "greatest living Realizer" along spiritual lines of development. As little chance as there is of the latter idea being true, it would at least partially avoid charges of hypocrisy against kw, for saying one thing publicly but another privately.

Of course, that would still not settle the question as to how "surrendering completely," even in a "mature" way, to an admitted "problematic [i.e., Jonestown-like], damn fool, fuck-up" (kw's words, all), could possibly be a good idea. And note again that all of those evaluations were given by Wilber himself well *prior* to his "deep, devotional bow" to the Master, above. Such behaviors could only have a psychological, never merely a "logical," basis and explanation.

So, too, for the following analysis from kw:

[Adi Da] makes a lot of mistakes. These are immediately re-interpreted as great teaching events, which is silly (Wilber, 1996a).

Such a regard, of course, completely overlooks the fact that, if one is truly "surrendered completely" to a guru-figure, there are no possible criteria which one could use to distinguish between valid "teaching events" and "mistakes" on his part. (Plus, Da has report-edly told his followers that he "can do no wrong" [Feuerstein, 1992].) Rather, it is all equally "divinely inspired," and all equally done "for the benefit of all sentient beings."

Wilber's own writings give no indication that he has ever been spiritually disciplined over an extended period of time in a "crazy wisdom" environment. (By "an extended period of time" is meant a minimum of six continuous months. At one point, he was consider-ing [1991] taking a three-year meditation retreat at an ashram run by Kalu Rinpoche, but evidently never actually did so.) He has at-tended *satsanga* at the feet of Adi Da on the Mountain of Atten-tion. But surely even he must realize that there is a huge differ-ence between spending a few days or weeks as a guest in such an environment, versus being trapped there for months or years.

Indeed, as to the difference between being in any such com-munity as a "star" versus as a long-term peon, Bailey (2003) ex-plained:

For most devotees, a visit to the [Sai Baba] ashram means sitting in the *darshan* lines looking on, wishing and hoping for interaction, whilst listening to the stories others tell. This is very different to being "in there"—seeing how things work behind the scenes.

The same is true, of course, of every other ashram, under every other spiritual leader under the sun:

Even journalists who would come to write exposés on the do-ings at [Rajneesh's ashram near] Antelope would come out feeling, *The place is really a nice place, those people are really fine people* (Strelley, 1987).

[A]t the center of Moonism is the requirement of secrecy ... we had heard only a carefully devised elementary lecture [when first visiting our daughter in Moon's community] (Underwood and Underwood, 1979).

[W]hen government visitors, doctors, even our attorney ... came to Jonestown we put on a tremendous show for them. The guests were wined and dined with foods we never got to eat. In fact, when they looked into our faces we really were happy because on these special occasions we, too, got better food and we worked only half a day (Layton, 1998).

The tours were entirely staged, with church members rehearsed in their roles, outfitted in borrowed clothes to look the part, and coached ahead of time on what to say.... If a visit went off successfully and the outsider went away impressed, Jones would switch to a new role. He would stand before the congregation and mock the visitor, imitating his or her voice, repeating questions asked and laughing at how the women visitors had brushed against him suggestively (Singer, 2003).

Well-meaning individuals thus duped even prior to Jones' flight to Guyana included Jerry Brown, activist Angela Davis, future San Francisco mayor Willie Brown, and President Carter's wife, Rosalyn. On the basis of similar "dog and pony" shows, Oregon journalist Kirk Braun (1984) wrote "a highly favorable book on ranch life" in Rajneeshpuram (Gordon, 1987). And astonishingly, one of the daughters of Congressman Leo Ryan—whose cold-blooded murder by Jones' men in Guyana precipitated the infamous cyanide poisonings—later became an ardent follower of Rajneesh, living in the Oregon ashram.

Contrast all that we have seen so far, then, with Wilber's (1983b; italics added) ridiculous presentation of his own limited, short-term experiences:

I have been a participant-observer in almost a dozen non-problematic new religious movements, Buddhist, Hindu, Taoist. In *none* of those groups was I ever subjected to any harsh degree of authoritarian pressure (discipline, yes, pressure, no). In fact, the authoritarian pressure in these groups never even equalled that which I experienced in graduate school in biochemistry. The masters in these groups were looked upon as great teachers, not big daddies, and their authority was always that of a *concerned physician,* not totem boss.

"Concerned physicians," though, do not typically tell you that, if you leave their care to see a different doctor, you will "suffer unbearable, subtle, continuous anguish, and disasters will pursue you like furies" (cf. Trungpa), etc. As the *Mill Valley Record* (Colin, et al., 1985) further reported:

> One woman says that repeated group lesbian sexual acts, involving dildos, took place under [Adi Da's] command as late as 1982. Another woman says she has sustained permanent cervical damage as a result of participation in similar incidents.

"Concerned physicians." And note again how, incredibly, Wilber's indefensible assertion that "'crazy wisdom' occurs in a very strict ethical atmosphere" was made in 1996, a full *decade* after news of Da's "problematic" (Wilber's word) alleged activities had become public. It also came well after Osel Tendzin's (Trungpa's successor) transmission of AIDS to his followers, knowing full well that he was infected with HIV but refraining from informing his sexual partners of that.

One may embark on any series of short-term "intensive retreats," experiencing grand spiritual realizations during those periods. That, however, again does not even *begin* to count, as far as perceiving the real pressures put on long-term, non-celebrity members of spiritual communities. To put it more flippantly: You may spend a couple of weeks in India, but that doesn't make you an East Indian. For, in Jung's terms, all the time you were there, you were "breathing bottled air," or seeing everything from within a pre-existing Western, rational perspective. Such a "vacation" cannot in any way be compared to growing up within the environment, or even to spending years or decades in it.

If all of that leaves one wondering what specific relationship Wilber has to Adi Da and his community:

> Wilber told me he was a "Friend" of the [Adi Da] group—a non-committed involvement (Lane, 1996).

> [T]o be a "Friend" of the Johannine Daist Communion one should contribute $70 or more and subscribe to *The Laughing Man Magazine* (Lane, 1996a).

It is, indeed, only from such a safe distance that one could make completely unrealistic, purely *theoretical* assertions such as the following:

> [T]he true *sangha* always *retains access to,* and retains an appropriate place for, rational inquiry, logical reflection, systematic study of other philosophical frameworks, and critical appraisal of its own teachings in light of related areas (Wilber, 1983b).

Note, however, that Adi Da's, Trungpa's and Cohen's communities were/are all undoubtedly "true *sanghas,*" by any reasonable definition, and certainly would have been such in Wilber's view. Yet, all indications are that in no way could the teachings be "critically appraised" in any of those environments without severe reported negative consequences:

> Overtly displayed skepticism [cf. "critical appraisal" or nonconformity] might be a barrier to entering the Vajrayana [in Trungpa's *sangha*]. One Seminarian drank a toast to Vajra hell at a party, was reported to the staff, and found himself questioned very closely before they would allow him to proceed.... I told my interviewer that if I had cause to leave the organization I would do so, and I did not believe the furies of Vajra hell would offer me anything to compare with the pain of divorce. This display of independence made me a doubtful candidate, and I had to pass a second interview (Butterfield, 1994).

> If you resisted Free John, it meant you were failing to live up to his teaching (Jaclyn Estes, in [Neary, 1985]).

Estes was formerly one of Da's "inner circle of wives," living in his community from 1974 to 1976.

Can there even be such a thing as a "true *sangha*" which allows "critical appraisal of its own teachings," as Wilber describes? The odds are definitely against it. For, consider the idea that all spiritual communities, indeed all religious beliefs, are pre-rational, by any sensible, reality-tested use of that term. That is, metaphysical and parapsychological claims consistently do not stand up to any sort of thorough questioning: proper skepticism simply causes the most cherished ideas to disintegrate. So, the only way to preserve the latter ideas is to disallow the former questioning;

which is, in practice, exactly what invariably happens in spiritual communities, including Wilber's own.

In any case, the *committed,* long-term residential relationship —evidently missing from Wilber's experience—under a guru-figure such as Da or Cohen is exactly where the *real* problems with "Rude Boy" behavior, and the associated isolation and authoritarian control, would start to show. Such a lack of long-term residence further avoids daily discipline to exactly the same extent as would one's following of an "Ascended Master," no longer present on the earthly plane, as is common in New Age circles. The positive aspect of each of those, however, is that you are then just bowing before an imaginary guru. Far worse to surrender your better judgment to someone of flesh and blood who has a great deal to gain from your unthinking obedience.

After being burned once with Da, however, Wilber has inexcusably gone back for more with Andrew Cohen. That is, he has gone back there via safely *endorsing* Cohen from a distance, as he did with Adi Da, without actually *living* under their respective disciplines. (Cohen proudly put his own grandiosity into print—offering glaring warning signs, for anyone who wished to see them—as early as 1992. Has Wilber still not read those early books, even while endorsing the more recent ones? Or, if he has read them, how could he imagine that Cohen's near-messianic view of himself would not find its way into his reported treatment of his disciples?)

To make that same gross mistake twice is, quite frankly, an indication that the same celebrated "rude" behavior is latently present within one's own psychology, and is simply looking for a vicarious outlet.

In any case, none of that lamentable behavior on Wilber's part could do anything to lower the regard given him by his friends and followers, or even touted by himself for himself:

> On a practical level, Wilber's greatest contribution may be as a critic of teachers, gurus, techniques, ideas, and systems that promise routes to encompassing truth but are in fact incomplete, misleading, or misguided. "I'm the guy," Wilber told me only half-jokingly, "who comes in after the party and tries to straighten up the mess" (Schwartz, 1996).

In any such self-appointed cleaning, however, one must take care that one does not accidentally knock over the half-empty bottles from the night before, or carelessly dump the ashtrays onto the floor, lest one create an even greater mess than one began with.

In the end, then, David Lane (1996) put it very well:

> When it comes to guru appraisements, Wilber is just plain naïve. He is as gullible as the rest of us and given his track record with Da perhaps more so.
>
> What is perhaps so worrisome about all of this, of course, is that Wilber does not show the kind of level-headed discrimination that is necessary to separate the wheat from the chaff. It would be one thing to admit to a bit of "greenness" (e.g., "Hey, I am a sucker when it comes to perfect masters"), but it is quite another to pose like you are a seasoned veteran of the guru wars.

KW is indeed no "veteran of the gurus wars." He is rather an inexcusable apologist for the reported actions of the likes of Da and Cohen. He has even been visited personally by cult-aware persons such as the renowned cult-exit counselor Steven Hassan, to no avail. You take seriously his foolish ideas on the value of "spiritual violence"—and his own proud practice of the techniques of manipulation he has learned from his "enlightened" heroes—only at your own peril.

And then there is the false humility:

> Ken jokes that "being called the foremost theorist in transpersonal psychology is like being called the tallest building in Kansas City" (in Wilber, 1991).

The above could be simply an unconvincing attempt at self-deprecation, or a posing at humility, meant to endear himself to an attractive woman. (The one to whom it was told actually ended up becoming Wilber's second wife.) Or, it could be a not-too-veiled shot at the unimpressive work of his "shorter building" peers in transpersonal/integral psychology and, more recently, the broader field of consciousness studies. Probably some of both. Regardless, Wilber need not have published the above observation, taken from his now-late wife's diaries, if he was uncomfortable with how it could be understood by others. And both of the above interpretations of subtext are completely predictable and reasonable, for anyone who wishes to look.

Horgan (2003a) then offers an observation regarding Wilber's overall attempts at being liked, with which one cannot easily argue:

> His self-deprecating asides [in *One Taste,* e.g., regarding his "world-famous" chili, "of which nobody took seconds"] seemed aimed only at making us admire his modesty.

Indeed, Wilber (1991) has given analyses of himself which could well be taken as substantiating Horgan's conclusions:

> I think everybody should love me, and when someone doesn't, I get nervous. So, as a child, I overcompensated like crazy. Class president, valedictorian, even captain of the football team. A frantic dance for acceptance, an attempt to have *everybody* love me.

If you wonder at where kw's subsequently paranoid, "if anybody loves me, they are sick" emphasis comes from, or how deeply rooted that is, you need puzzle no longer: it is just the flip-side of the same pattern, and thus entirely predictable.

More recently, and with far less of an attempt at false humility than in his "tallest building in Kansas City" days, Wilber (2003a) has stated his own attitude toward at least one of his critics, as follows:

> I'm sure if [Hans-Willi] Weis would read my work in this area [of authoritarian control and the like in New Age movements, on which points Wilber is consistently and *wildly* wrong, as in his dangerously foolish *Spiritual Choices* book] that he could find something to hate about it, too, and we are all eagerly looking forward to his next round of criticism, although I'm sure that I will be forgiven if I don't respond, since I might have more important things to do, like feed my goldfish.

One might take that condescending attempt at humor as an implicit admission by Wilber that, in other cases too, when he has disagreed with but not responded to other authors' ideas, it was simply because he had "more important things to do." That is, they did not merit a response from him.

How, then, would such a person be likely to react if he were to suddenly find himself on the receiving end of the same behavior, in apparently being ignored until he went away? Would he perhaps unconsciously take that behavior as being driven by the same motivations as he himself has openly admitted to possessing? That is, would he take it as his colleagues evidently feeling that they had more important things to do than to waste time explaining things to him?

Would he then perhaps feel sufficiently insulted by that as to periodically lash out at the people who have not given him his due, in the form of a response—any response? (Without receiving an answer, after all, one feels as though one does not exist in the other person's world. As Jean-Paul Sartre put it, "I am seen: therefore I am.")

Would such a long-term lack of response further perhaps even leave him feeling confident that he could lash out in unprovoked nastiness, without having to worry about the targets of his insults hitting back? (As Matsakis [1996] observed in a different context, in discussing "express[ing] your anger in a letter," never to be mailed: you "can be as nasty as you want without worrying about it backfiring on you.")

Would that not account for his continuing, and wholly unprovoked, mistreatment of the late David Bohm, as detailed in this book's appendix?

Interestingly, by Wilber's own (1991) admission:

[W]hen fear overcomes me, my ordinary lightness of outlook ... degenerates into sarcasm and snideness, a biting bitterness toward those around me—not because I am snide by nature, but because I am afraid.

Bohm's Nobel-caliber ideas would not have been felt by Wilber to fearfully threaten his own place in the world, had he properly understood them—except in that anyone doing superior work to his own, as Bohm was performing even while Wilber himself was literally still in kindergarten, could have displaced him from his high position as the "Einstein of consciousness research." Having thus grossly misunderstood even the popularized versions of that brilliance, though, the fearful Wilber has, predictably, treated Bohm (and his memory) with nothing but unkindness.

Do you imagine, then, that he would behave any more nobly toward his contemporary peers—or friends, or lovers—were they to equally threaten his high place in the integral world by doing far superior work to his own? Or, were they even just to fail to give him unconditional support, thus putting themselves at risk of being disowned from his integral world.

Or would he more likely misrepresent their work as unapologetically and insultingly as he has done of Bohm's, thereby "nudging them out of the picture"? And what friends might then stand by his side to claim, even years after the fact, that he had committed no such misrepresentation, even when the incontrovertible facts say exactly the opposite?

(Of course, we already saw confirmation of all that in the behaviors of Wilber and his followers during his "Wyatt Earpy" period.)

Whether one is "captain of the football team" or the "Einstein of consciousness research," the potential loss of that valued status would bring great fear to the surface. That is so, just as surely as the original gaining of the position, in high school as in middle or old age, would be done with at least the subconscious goal of having "everybody love you."

CHAPTER XI

# CARGO CULT PHILOSOPHY

People like von Daniken [re: UFOs] and Velikovsky say a lot of things that seem quite plausible to the layman, but scientists with specialized knowledge in the relevant fields treat them as a joke. Is Wilber the philosophical equivalent of such figures?

MANY YEARS AGO, RICHARD FEYNMAN (1989) offered an insightful critique of the "cargo cult science" into which Wilber's work falls so squarely:

[T]here is one feature I notice that is generally missing in cargo cult science. That is the idea that we all hope you have learned in studying science in school—we never say explicitly what this is, but just hope that you catch on by all the examples of scientific investigation. It is interesting, therefore, to bring it out now and speak of it explicitly. **It's a kind of scientific integrity, a principle of scientific thought that corresponds to a kind of utter honesty—a kind of leaning over backwards.** For example, if you're doing an

experiment, you should report everything that you think
might make it invalid—not only what you think is right
about it: other causes that could possibly explain your results; and things you thought of that you've eliminated by
some other experiment, and how they worked—to make sure
the other fellow can tell they have been eliminated.

Details that could throw doubt on your interpretation
must be given, if you know them. You must do the best you
can—if you know anything at all wrong, or possibly wrong—
to explain it. If you make a theory, for example, and adver-
tise it, or put it out, then you must also put down all the
facts that disagree with it, as well as those that agree with
it. There is also a more subtle problem. When you have put a
lot of ideas together to make an elaborate theory, you want
to make sure, when explaining what it fits, that those things
it fits are not just the things that gave you the idea for the
theory; but that the finished theory makes something else
come out right, in addition.

In summary, the idea is to give all of the information to
help others to judge the value of your contribution; not just
the information that leads to judgment in one particular direction or another....

We've learned from experience that the truth will come
out. Other experimenters will repeat your experiment and
find out whether you were wrong or right. Nature's phenomena will agree or they'll disagree with your theory. And, although you may gain some temporary fame and excitement,
you will not gain a good reputation as a scientist if you ha-
ven't tried to be very careful in this kind of work. And it's
this type of integrity, this kind of care not to fool yourself,
that is missing to a large extent in much of the research in
cargo cult science.

Ken Wilber may have garnered some "temporary fame and excitement" for his "cargo cult philosophy"—having always "bent over
backwards" in exactly the wrong way, to *obfuscate/ignore* facts
which did not mesh with his "theories." But that "success" is fairly
meaningless, being achieved only in a field of "scholarship" popu-
lated by admirers who simply don't know any better, and who will
fight their critics, tooth and nail, should the latter try to present
them with thorough research which utterly discredits their system
of beliefs. The truth will indeed come out. And, in the end, the

world will know Wilber for the foolish, authoritarian pretender he has always been.

The idea that kw may actually be the "Velikovsky of consciousness research" may be funny, but it is no joke. As Robert Carroll (2005b) noted about Velikovsky, though: "That is not to say that his work is not an impressive exercise and demonstration of ingenuity and erudition [i.e., in imaginative "theorizing" and the taking of mere coincidences as if they indicated deep, underlying connections]. It is very impressive [though nonetheless hopelessly wrong], but it isn't science. It isn't even history."

Wilber's presentation of the various disciplines and perspectives which (he claims) support his integral theories, too, is so distorted and regularly false that it "isn't even history."

Less charitably, Velikovsky's former associate Leroy Ellenberger observed: "The less one knows about science, the more plausible Velikovsky's scenario appears." And, in the words of Michael Friedlander: "I would not trust any alleged citation by Velikovsky without checking the original printed sources."

Or, consider this: "Velikovsky interprets, adds, and deletes liberally while insisting he is adhering literally to the evidence.... Given such an array of data and freedom to interpret, the legends can be made to fit any theory."

Or this: "[W]hen a book contains obvious incompetencies that can be spotted just at random, you don't need to read the whole thing to conclude it's junk."

Or this: "[T]he New York literary world considered Velikovsky a genius on par with 'Einstein, Newton, Darwin and Freud.'"

Or, finally, this: "[T]here can be no denying the scientific indifference and incompetence of Velikovsky."

Do those critiques remind you of anyone else's work?

But Velikovsky [like Wilber] makes it all look so *consistent*. Surely he couldn't put all those legends together so neatly unless his theory was true? Variations on this theme come up with just about every type of pseudoscience. The startling truth is that theories that hang together pretty well logically and are reasonably consistent with most of the evidence are a dime a dozen in science. **It's easy—anyone can construct one**. The key to the problem lies in the qualifiers "pretty well," "reasonably consistent," and "most of the evidence." The difference between a mediocre theory and a good one is that the good theory is as nearly as possible *entirely consistent* with *all* the evidence. You can make any theory look good if you are free to disregard or rearrange key bits of evidence (Dutch, 2001).

Wilber has, of course, traded on that fact for his entire career.

Nevertheless, taking multiple perspectives on reality, as kw encourages, is indeed valuable. And endorsing any philosophy or religion while listening to skeptical arguments against it is itself a multi-perspectival viewpoint.

Equally, though, following the evidence, while still hoping that even the most wide-eyed of spiritual claims will turn out, upon competent testing, to be true, is also multi-perspectival.

In the former route, you end up believing in a wide variety of fairy tales, and discounting their consistent failure to show their purported effects in properly controlled studies as a mere temporary setback or a shortcoming of "skeptical-materialistic science." You will also, if history and psychology are any guide, simultaneously elevate the "false positives" of improperly performed studies to the status of "best evidence"—happy to believe whatever you wish until it is "disproved," in spite of the difficulty/impossibility of proving a negative. (That is, the impossibility of proving that leprechauns don't exist, for example.)

In the latter route, by contrast, you simply resolve to face reality, whatever it may turn out to be, even while still hoping that, by some phenomenal coincidence, the universe may yet turn out to have a point to its existence after all.

Religion/spirituality benefits greatly from the former, "multi-perspectival believer" approach; the greatest discoveries in science, by contrast, have consistently been made by people who took the latter.

If you really care about having your beliefs correspond to reality, you have to be prepared to face, and act on, the possibility that they don't.

And, if you think you can take the "good" from the integral perspective, for example, and leave the rest behind, consider this: Every point on which I, or anyone else, has debunked Ken Wilber's claims, was at one time supposedly part of what was worth saving from his ideas.

Further, as far as practice goes: Do you really need a formal philosophy or an integration of the current schools of thought in order to know enough to lead a balanced life, or to justify living that way to yourself? (You know: Exercise, relaxation, good food but not too much of it, read a good book with proper footnoting now and then, don't believe everything you're told by persons who stand to gain from your willing obedience, etc.) If you do, here's one:

> We should consider every day lost on which we have not danced at least once.

You know who said that? Friedrich Nietzsche—a *real* philosopher, who didn't need to substitute fairy tales for reality and then pretend that that was an improvement rooted in his own exalted "second-tier spiritual realization."

Can one then claim that there is no need to integrate the various approaches in the field of consciousness studies, or at least to point out the first- and third-person approaches that divide it? Surely, listing the current schools of thought, and the attempt, by Wilber and others, to arrange them in some kind of order, can only help?

As a first point, it is exactly the *attempt* to find order in all those phenomena *without having any idea about how to separate the real ones from the imaginary ones* that has created the integral mess in the first place. Thus, the "theorists" give equal weight to the "effectiveness" of long-ago debunked homeopathy and acupuncture, and to the "proven" efficacy of meditation in advancing psychological stage-growth, as they give to a *real* process of evolution (which has to be utterly misrepresented in order to fit into their "theories"). But where, in life, do we get marks simply for "attempting" things, much less for giving the false impression of success by dishonestly/selectively ignoring uncomplimentary, contrary information?

And, ironically, it is exactly the combination of third-person and first-person approaches, in the use of basic statistics and double-blind settings to evaluate claims of the abilities to see auras or to do astral travel, for example, that has provided the most evidence that such purported abilities are unlikely to be real.

Plus, you cannot do anything resembling science by "including everything" now, and only later weeding out the phenomena that don't actually exist. Consequently, until you have thoroughly determined what the "best evidence" that needs to be explained actually is, your theories are inherently going to be "dime a dozen" ones, which fit "pretty well" with whatever you hope may exist in the physical and transpersonal worlds. When exactly that same approach is being taken in the attempt to arrange current schools of thought into some kind of order, one truly doesn't even need to read the "breakthrough" publications in order to know that they are not going to stand up to questioning.

Further, proper theories in any field don't merely explain existing phenomena and predict new ones. Rather, *they also "disallow" claimed phenomena which have failed to show themselves in proper testing.* How is the integral "we'll weed it out later" approach to a "Theory of Everything" ever going to accomplish the latter point? Even in principle, it cannot.

Of course, for people with an interest in such things, there will always be at least a psychological need for such attempts at integration. But Wilber (and at least 80% of his critics, and at least 99% of his followers) woefully lack the knowledge to effect that integration, or even to properly critique others' attempts at it. (That knowledge-base would cover original sources, along with one's understanding *and applying* of the fact that literally nothing of what one might like to believe about the hoped-for transpersonal aspects of reality has ever showed itself in any properly conducted and repeated testing.)

Further, since the integral community as a whole is blatantly unable to recognize false attempts at such integration even when the flaws are enumerated in precise detail, it doesn't have a prayer of recognizing true ones, either. Its members simply won't know the difference.

Still, it is never an all-or-nothing proposition. Is the attempt to put current schools of thought into some kind of order a good thing, at least in principle? Of course it is. Has any good come out of it? Of course. Has any bad come out of it? Yes, quite a lot actually. Does integral philosophy do more harm than good? Based on lost productivity, the psychotic side-effects of meditation, and the like, I would say yes, it does significantly more harm than good; notwithstanding that, like all "opiates of the masses," it does serve a social and salvational function for the in-group.

The problem with integral/spiritual pursuits is that they are never content to be mere theories; they always want to be *applied* to real lives. While that may *sound* like a good idea, it's exactly in the applying that all the worst damage is done.

CHAPTER XII

# THE EINSTEIN OF P.R.

AFTER ALL THIS, one may begin to wonder where the "Einstein of consciousness" title got started, with regard to Ken Wilber.

It turns out that the original source of the undeserved appellation was John White (1997b). As per his "Foreword to the Twentieth-Anniversary Edition" of *The Spectrum of Consciousness*, reproduced in Volume One of Wilber's *Collected Works*:

> Altogether, Wilber's spiritual understanding, creativity, scholarship and literary competence make him, **as I said in an early review of his work, the much-needed Einstein of consciousness research**. "Much-needed" because since the Psychedelic Sixties, there has been burgeoning interest in higher states of consciousness, noetics and allied subjects.

White was Wilber's literary agent for his (1977) *The Spectrum of Consciousness*; kw actually dedicated the book to him. Thus, White stood to benefit financially in direct proportion to the sales of that book.

That something which began as little more than self-serving P.R. could have since become nearly "accepted wisdom," in no small part through simple consumer gullibility, peer ignorance, and the force of repetition from authorities and others in the field, is quite astonishing, is it not?

139

Interestingly, John White is also, by his own (1997) testimony, one of the deeply "enlightened" ones gracing this Earth:

> My exceptional human experience (EHE) is the experience of God-realization.... I entered that [*sahaj samadhi*] state permanently in 1979.

Wilber has been called the "Einstein of consciousness research"? Yes, indeed he has. But more accurately, he has been called the "Einstein of consciousness research" *by his own literary agent.*

In kw's enlightenment.com interview, as given in his (2001d) *Speaking of Everything,* he further commented on the aftereffects of having written his first book in his early twenties:

> I went through a period of, kind of inflation and unbalance, because so many projections are put on you that you are both demonic—I'm much more [*sic*] demonic than some people would think I am—and also there are positive projections going on. And what tends to happen is that some way, sooner or later, you really have to address that.... So even somebody who is kind of slow, like me, in that area, I'm pretty okay....

But is Wilber really "pretty okay" in terms of his "inflation and unbalance"? Particularly given that his "Wyatt Earpy" behaviors read like a textbook case of clinical narcissism, while his professional activities and even his method of working test the limits of academic incompetence:

> I don't take notes. I don't have notebooks. I work on a computer and that's it.... I don't know why this is so, but it is almost like idiot savant.... I've read at least a Ph.D. level in 23 disciplines....
>
> I also have an idiot savant level of pattern recognition.... Because I have that pattern recognition, if I would read like Jane Loevinger and then two years later read Eric Yance and years later read Robert Kegan or something, I would instantly see how they fit (Wilber, 2007).

But, what happens when you are not merely superficially-read across a large number of fields, but actually go back to Wilber's original sources, to verify the support which he claims from them? Well, you consistently find that he has, provably, quite unconscionably misrepresented those same fields in order to make them "fit" with what he wants the "truth" to be. Conversely, without that brutal misrepresentation of the facts, he could again never have (falsely) "integrated" all of the fields of knowledge which he pretends to have covered.

Consider Wilber's own (2006) claims regarding his purported understanding of postmodernism:

> Not only did I grok what the postmodernists were saying, I have given, in dozens of writings, what numerous experts and specialists in the field (including experts on Foucault, Derrida, Lyotard, among others) have called some of the best, and in a few instances, THE best, treatment of these topics.

By contrast, Desilet (2007) observes, in his "Misunderstanding Derrida and Postmodernism":

> At an *Integral Spirituality* book signing in Boulder (November, 2006) Ken Wilber and I had a brief exchange about postmodernism and specifically his understanding of Derrida....
>
> Wilber claimed that Derrida himself came to understand the overstatement of his case and in an interview published in *Positions* (1981) reversed himself by acknowledging the transcendental signifier/signified's necessary role in language....
>
> Wilber's reading is a bad misreading. In fact, it is a misreading that twists what Derrida says into its opposite....
>
> Wilber [further] misses a crucial part of the Derridean deconstructive critique of understanding, signification, and communication....
>
> Wilber's understanding of postmodernism remains short-sighted as he continues to insist that it does not imply what Derrida believes it implies....
>
> Despite his sophistication, Wilber appears to have missed the point of deconstructive postmodernism.

Much of Wilber's penchant for provable fabrication and misrepresentation becomes readily understandable if one considers the following ideas, as related in David Berreby's (2005) *Us and Them:*

Sir Frederic Charles Bartlett ... studied memory with a simple experimental procedure. He would ask his students to read a folktale, wait a few hours or a few days, and then re-tell it.

He was careful to select a story that they had never heard before. (It came from anthropological accounts of the Kathlamet people of Oregon.) As you might expect, the student versions left out many details. When they did recall something, they often changed it to make it more familiar. (For instance, they made "peanut" into the more British "acorn" and described paddle-wielding warriors as "rowing" their canoe, the way proper English undergraduates would handle a scull.) The students also added details that weren't in the original. Where the story read "That Indian has been hit," some recalled an Indian being killed, others an Indian being hit by an arrow. Recalling a warrior in the tale who says he will not go into combat because his relatives don't know where he is, "but you may go," many of Bartlett's volunteers added an explanation, like "you have no one to expect you," or "you have no parents."

The students were unaware that some of their "memories" were actually alterations or additions. They imagined they were simply recalling what they had read. It felt so right that they did not see where the story stopped and their own contribution began.

Bartlett decided the students were confident about their memories because they came to the story with a ready-made mental map. When they read about Indian warriors, they thought of arrows....

Once the students had seen enough detail to call up the relevant map, a pattern seemed to complete itself in their minds, and they felt no difference between what they had learned from the outside world and what they had supplied.

One can easily apply that firmly established psychological principle to the integral/AQAL fairy tales told by Wilber. And, having done so, one need wonder no longer at how the man can add, delete and modify "facts" at will, always in accord with his "ready-made mental maps," while simultaneously proudly touting his "idiot savant" method of *not taking notes* from the books he reads, in his drastically inadequate method of "research." All the while "feeling no difference" between objective facts, and the fabrications which he presents as being "real."

More realistically than kw's complimentary self-evaluations, then:

> [P]erhaps it is the ironic fate of those striving toward universality and integration, to end up being the most marginal and idiosyncratic cranks (in Boucher, 2005).

Even having done all of this debunking, though, note that Wilber is, still, truly the best which transpersonal psychology and integral studies have to argue for the validity of their viewpoints and "theories." Further, he still has the support of the vast majority of "experts" in the field, even after being thoroughly discredited in his professional work.

Even just at the level directly below kw's "brilliant" contributions, respected founding members of his Integral Institute include:

- Deepak Chopra, former follower of the Maharishi, who was celebrated by *Time* magazine in 1999 as ostensibly being "the poet-prophet of alternative medicine." Of *The Marriage of Sense and Soul,* Chopra said: "Ken Wilber is one of the most important pioneers in the field of consciousness in this century. I regard him as my mentor.... Read everything he writes—it will change your life." In return, Wilber (2006e) feted Chopra as purportedly being "a fine scholar with a searching intellect"

- Gary Schwartz, the University of Arizona researcher who sincerely believes, as per his *Afterlife Experiments* (2002), that the claimed mediums he has tested are talking to the dead. However, as Ray Hyman (2003) has noted, "Probably no other extended program in psychical research deviates so much from accepted norms of scientific methodology as [Schwartz's] does"

- Larry Dossey, whose ideas on "nonlocal mind" and the role of spirituality and prayer in healthcare have greatly influenced the spread of alternative medicine

- Michael Lerner, author of *The Politics of Meaning.* Lerner was briefly dubbed the "guru of the White House" during the Clinton administration, and considers Wilber to be a "great mind," whose "brilliance pours out on every page" of his (*One Taste*) journals

- Joe Firmage, a Silicon Valley software entrepreneur who initially endowed the Integral Institute in 1997, to the tune of a full million dollars. Shortly thereafter, Firmage reportedly "revealed his conviction that some UFOs are extraterrestrial visitors" (Klass, 2000)

- Warren Bennis, author of over twenty-five books on leadership, and advisor to four past U.S. presidents. Bennis has been called the "Dean of Leadership Gurus" by *Forbes* magazine

- Nathaniel Branden—Ayn Rand's "intellectual heir," to whom *Atlas Shrugged* was dedicated. (The book itself was the "greatest human achievement in the history of the world," according to Rand and Branden.) Together, they encouraged followers of Rand to consider them as being "the two greatest intellects on the planet." By Branden's own website testimony, he "has done more, perhaps, than any other theorist to awaken America's consciousness to the importance of self-esteem to human well-being"

- Michael Murphy, co-founder of the famed New Age Esalen Institute. Murphy genuinely believes (1992) that the East Indian sage Ramakrishna's spine lengthened during his period of spiritual discipline. He also appears to consider (1998) the long-debunked "thought photography" of Ted Serios to be a genuine parapsychological phenomenon

- Roger Walsh, who teaches philosophy and other subjects at the University of California at Irvine. He is also a member of the Board of Editors for both *The Journal of Transpersonal Psychology* and the *Journal of Consciousness Studies.* Together with his wife Frances Vaughan, Walsh (1988) edited a book of selections from Helen Schucman's *A Course in Miracles* (ACIM)—attempted pithy sermons which were purportedly channeled from Jesus Christ in the mid-1960s. Walsh and Vaughan's (1993) anthology, *Paths Beyond Ego,* has a foreword written by UFOlogist John E. Mack. In Walsh's opinion, "Ken Wilber is one of the greatest philosophers of this century and arguably the greatest theoretical psychologist of all time"

- Robert Thurman, named as one of *Time* magazine's twenty-five most influential people in 1997, and viewed as "America's number one Buddhist" by the *New York Times.* Also, father of Hollywood goddess Uma. Both Thurman and the Dalai Lama endorsed Deepak Chopra's (2000) book, *How to Know God,* as did Ken Wilber and the spoon-bending Uri Geller. Thurman called it the "most important book about God for our times." He has also released two (1999, 2000) recordings of dialogs between himself and Chopra

- Marilyn Schlitz, purported astral-voyaging remote-viewer of distant sites. Champion, with Dean Radin, of ganzfeld experiments (debunked in [Carroll, 2005d]) as dubious proof of the existence of psi phenomena. Director of Research at the Institute of Noetic Sciences. Her book *Consciousness and Healing: Integral Approaches to Mind-Body Medicine,* contains contributions by Chopra and Dossey, and a foreword by Wilber

- The gurus Andrew Cohen, Richard Baker (formerly of the San Francisco Zen Center) and Saniel Bonder, the latter of whom co-edited Adi Da's *Garbage and the Goddess,* wherein his claim of manifesting the "miraculous corona" is made

- Tony Robbins, fire-walking father of the "life coaching industry," and practitioner of Neuro-Linguistic Programming. Q-Links have also apparently been offered for sale at Robbins' seminars (Randi, 2002a)

- "Integral artists" Stuart Davis and Ed Kowalczyk, the latter being the lead singer for the group Live. Kowalczyk had earlier named his pet turtle "Murti," after the ex-Theosophical sage Krishnamurti, and was "transported into a state of wonderment and awe" by at least one of Adi Da's books

- Bob Richards (co-founder of Clarus, makers of the Q-Link pendant)

- Keith Thompson, referenced earlier in terms of de Quincey's experiences with the so-called Wilber police

- Brian Van der Horst, quoted at the beginning of Chapter II for his "Light in the Wilberness" insights

More surprisingly, the noted atheist Sam Harris has guested on Wilber's Integral Naked bully-pulpit forum. He further spoke complimentarily of kw's ideas in the endnotes to his own (2003) *The End of Faith,* saying:

[A] process of increasing individuation clearly occurs from birth onward. See K. Wilber, *Sex, Ecology, Spirituality* (Boston: Shambhala, 1995), for a criticism of the false equation between what he calls the *pre-rational* and the *trans-rational*. As Wilber points out, there is no reason to romanticize childhood in spiritual terms. Indeed, if our children appear to inhabit the kingdom of heaven, why stop with them? We might as well direct our envy at our primate cousins, for they—when they are not too overcome by the pleasures of cannibalism, gang rape, and infanticide to seem so—are the most gleeful children of all.

More generically, Harris dubiously averred, in the same endnotes:

[T]he future looks rather like the past.... We may live to see the technological perfection of all the visionary strands of traditional mysticism: shamanism (Siberian or South American), Gnosticism, Kabbalah, Hermetism and its magical Renaissance spawn (Hermeticism), and all the other Byzantine paths whereby man has sought the Other in every guise of its conception. But all these approaches to spirituality are born of a longing for esoteric knowledge and a desire to excavate the visionary state of the mind—in dreams, or trance, or psychedelic swoon—in search of the sacred. While I have no doubt that remarkable experiences are lying in wait for the initiate down each of these byways, the fact that consciousness is always the prior context and condition of every visionary experience is a great clarifying truth....

Harris also spoke positively of the psychedelic-fueled, hallucinatory "exquisite ravings" of Terence McKenna, in the same book.

As the *real rationalist* Meera Nanda (2003) then rightly noted:

Sam Harris is not all that far apart from Mahesh Yogi, Deepak Chopra and others who claim that spiritual practitioners have the most objective view of the world because they can see it "directly," just the way it is, completely "shorn of the self," and the many biases and dogmas that "I-ness" brings....

He loads spiritual practices with metaphysical baggage, all the while claiming to stand up for reason and evidence. By the end of the book, I could not help thinking of him as a Trojan horse for the New Age.

In contrast to Harris' muddle-headed approach, the philosopher and atheist Daniel Dennett

> does *not* dismiss the value of studying mystical experiences for either understanding how our brains compose our sense of self, or for personally helping one to achieve a sense of peace and contentment. In fact, Dennett said, he himself meditates and finds it very beneficial. He just disagrees that it gives someone insight into the nature of how the entire universe works, vs. into the nature of how the mind works. People who have spent years and years meditating don't come up with anything interesting beyond themselves (in Myers, 2007).

In any field of human knowledge, if one can thoroughly debunk the work of the "best" practitioners, one need hardly bother with taking the lesser lights seriously. For, not only are the latter's contributions to transpersonal/integral studies "not as good" as Wilber's, but in endorsing his work, either explicitly or through their founding membership in I-I, they have equally showed themselves to be unable to recognize provable fabrications even in their own fields of supposed expertise. And if the leading members in any field cannot tell the difference, there, you may be confident that the less-noteworthy followers cannot, either.

So if, after all of this, you still believe that Ken Wilber's vaunted philosophy and life's work are more than just the New Age effusions of an unconscionable, deluded/hallucinatory bullshit artist with little grasp on truth or reality, whose ideas are more than a profoundly negative, pre-rational force in the evolution of the species, and who has learned well from his reportedly abusive heroes how to manipulate others into thinking that the less they question his ideas the more "second tier" they are ... well, good luck to you.

You're going to need it.

> For years I was a fan of Ken Wilber, with emphasis on the word fan against another, preferable word: student. Instead of reading Wilber, a la Kant, as someone with ideas to be considered and argued with, I came to read him as the definitive authority on reality....
>
> Over the last several years, Wilber and his fans have become so fluent in the language of Integral, Integral-this and Integral-that, that they have effectively created an in-

group/out-group scenario reminiscent of the blue meme's good and evil, that they are so (rightly) critical of. You're either for Integral or against it. (And if you have a different definition of Integral, it's wrong....)

Unfortunately, instead of engaging critics and showing some humility, Wilber is further insulating all things Integral. And the whole movement around him now appears destined to become, isolated as it is, a cult, and soon after, lose whatever relevance it may have had in the scholarly world (Parker, 2007).

# APPENDIX

## WILBER AND BOHM: AN ANALYSIS OF
## THE PROBLEMS WITH KEN WILBER'S
## "REFUTATIONS" OF DAVID BOHM'S IDEAS


Nobody is capable of producing 100% error—nobody is smart enough to be wrong all the time (Wilber, 1999).


IN KEN WILBER'S *THE EYE OF SPIRIT* (1998), prefacing his criticism of Jenny Wade's (1996) appropriation of physicist David Bohm's "implicate order"-related ideas for her "holonomic" theory of consciousness, we find the following assertion:

> Bohm himself tended to realize the indefensible nature of his position, and for a while he went through an awkward period of adding implicate levels. There was the implicate level, then the super-implicate level, then at one point, a super-super-implicate level. And all of this, of course, was claiming to be based on empirical findings in physics!
>
> I published [1982] a strong criticism of Bohm's position, which has never been answered by him or any of [his] followers....
>
> Until this critique is even vaguely answered, I believe we must consider Bohm's theory to be refuted. And, anyway,

149

over the last decade and a half it has generally fallen into widespread disrepute (and it has no support whatsoever from recent physics).

In reprint (e.g., third) editions, "indefensible nature" has become "inadequate nature"; "is even vaguely answered" has become "is answered"; "theory to be refuted" has become "theory to be suspect"; and "no support whatsoever from recent physics" has become "little support from most physicists."

So presumably, in the interim, someone did give a "vague answer" to Wilber's critique, pointing out to him that Bohm's ideas were not quite as "indefensible" as kw would have imagined them to be. Also, that his objections to that reformulation of quantum theory, based in its apparent failure to accommodate mysticism's hypothetical Great Chain of Being—i.e., the purported hierarchy of causal, astral, and physical realities and states of consciousness—did not entirely "refute" it. And, that his characterization of its ostensible lack of support from real physics and physicists, too, was overblown.

I will be addressing Wilber's original critique, rather than his subsequently toned-down version of the same, in what follows. For, I do not believe that any of us should be required to purchase or slog through every new edition of each of kw's repetitive books, just to see how he has tried to soften his previous bold misrepresentations of other people's ideas. The conclusions here will stand firm, regardless. Plus, as we shall see, Wilber's own attitude toward Bohm's work, and corresponding attempts to easily dismiss it, have not improved at all in his other writings since then.

To begin, then, we note that the primary points in Bohm's fully developed ontological/causal/deterministic formulation of quantum theory, in terms of its relation to "holographic paradigms" and for distinguishing it from the orthodox indeterministic theory, are the following:

1. The existence of an "explicate order," comprised of any and all observable matter, whether it be Newtonian or quantum; and the corresponding existence of an "implicate order," of diffused wave-representations of matter overlapping one another, from which the explicate order of apparently separate particles arises

2. The existence of a "super-implicate order," as a "super-information field of the whole universe ... which organizes the first level [of the implicate and explicate orders] into various structures" (Bohm, in [Weber, 1986])

3. A "holographic" or "holomovement" nature to the universe, in which every element of space and matter potentially contains information about the whole universe

We will examine each of those components (plus Bohm's related "quantum potential") in turn. In doing so we shall find, simply by comparing "what Wilber said" to "what Bohm said," that Wilber has grossly misrepresented each of the three points above.

## 1. THE EXPLICATE AND IMPLICATE ORDERS

We are probably all familiar with Bohm's colloquial "ink-drop in glycerine" analogy, utilized toward his explanation of the implicate order in his formulation of quantum theory. If not, the relevant device consists of two concentric glass cylinders, with glycerine between them, and drops of insoluble ink being placed into the glycerine as the outer cylinder is turned. With that turning,

the droplet is drawn out [or "implicated" into the glycerine] into a fine thread-like form that eventually becomes invisible. When the cylinder is turned in the opposite direction the thread-form draws back and suddenly becomes visible [or "explicated"] as a droplet essentially the same as the one that was there originally (Bohm, 1980).

The relation of the often-misunderstood implicate order to the explicate order could also be summarized as follows:

[Imagine] a wave that comes to focus in a small region of space and then disperses. This is followed by another similar wave that focuses in a slightly different position, then by another and another and so on indefinitely until a "track" is formed that resembles the path of a particle. Indeed the particles of physics are more like these dynamic structures, which are always grounded in the whole from which they unfold and into which they enfold, than like little billiard balls that are grounded only in their own localized forms (Bohm and Peat, 1987).

That contraction/unfoldment and subsequent dispersion/enfoldment, with the particle being visible/explicated only when its wave-energy is highly concentrated at the transition between those two processes, is exactly the means by which the implicate order manifests as the explicate order. The explicate order is thus a subset of the implicate order. That is, the two orders are not mutually exclusive, as Bohm himself confirmed:

> [T]he explicate order itself may be obtainable from the implicate order as a special and determinate sub-order [i.e., a subset] that is contained within it (in Hiley and Peat, 1987).

> Up till now we have contrasted implicate and explicate orders, treating them as separate and distinct, but ... the explicate order can be regarded as a *particular or distinguished case* [i.e., a subset] *of a more general set of implicate orders from which latter it can be derived* [italics added]. What distinguishes the explicate order is that what is thus derived is a set of recurrent and relatively stable elements that are *outside* of each other (Bohm, 1980).

Wilber (1982), however, has offered a different, and incorrect, understanding of what Bohm has stated so clearly above:

> Some writers use the implicate order as a metaphor ... of transcendence. That is, the implicate realm is used as a metaphor of *higher-order* wholeness or unity, referring, presumably, to such levels as the subtle or causal.... The difficulty is that, as originally explained by Bohm for the realm of *physis,* the explicate and implicate "entities" are *mutually exclusive* [italics added]. The "ink-drop" particle is either unfolded and manifest (explicate) or it is enfolded and unmanifest (implicate). It cannot be both at the same time....
>
> All of which is fine for the dimension of *physis*. But truly higher levels are not mutually exclusive with lower ones— the higher, as we said, transcend but include the lower.

Of course, "disproving the [ink-drop] analogy" would obviously not necessarily say anything about the actual implicate and explicate orders of quantum theory. Even aside from that, however, it is not clear where the assertion that Bohm had "originally explained" that the implicate and explicate entities (and thus orders) were "mutually exclusive" could have come from, other than a disturbing lack of understanding, on Wilber's part, of both the analogy and the actual quantum orders themselves. For, we note that Bohm, by 1980, had already published his explicit statement, quoted earlier, that the explicate order is a "particular or distinguished case" or a *subset* of the implicate, i.e., that they are *not* mutually exclusive. Bohm's (1980) work, where that statement can be found, is actually included in the bibliography of Wilber (1998)—though being mis-dated there as from 1973, the year of publication of one of the papers which later became a chapter in that book. And it is again in that 1998 book where kw's assertion of "unanswered refutation" is given.

Much of Wilber's (1982) critique, including the block quote immediately above, was actually written in 1979. (Other interview-related parts pertaining to that critique have their original copyright from 1981.) That, however, still does not explain (or provide any excuse for) why Wilber did not correct those significant mis-statements prior to their collected 1982 publication. Nor does it account for why he has not issued relevant written statements of correction in any of his many publications in the decades since then.

The idea of the enfolding and unfolding of the implicate and explicate orders in physics has its mathematical basis in the "Green's function" of quantum wave mechanics (or via the "unitary transformation" in Heisenberg's matrix formulation). As Bohm notes (in Hiley and Peat, 1987):

> [W]hen I thought of the mathematical form of the quantum theory (with its matrix operations and Green's functions), I perceived that this too described just a movement of enfold-ment and unfoldment of the wave function. So the thought occurred to me: perhaps the movement of enfoldment and unfoldment is universal, while the extended and separate forms that we commonly see in experience are relatively sta-ble and independent patterns, maintained by a constant un-derlying movement of enfoldment and unfoldment. This lat-ter I called the *holomovement*.

> In the usual way of thinking, something like an implicate or-der is tacitly acknowledged, but it is not regarded as having any fundamental significance. For example, processes of en-foldment, such as those described by the Green's function, are assumed to be just convenient ways of analyzing what is

basically a movement in the explicate order, in which waves are transmitted continuously through a purely local contact of fields that are only infinitesimal distances from each other. In essence, however, the main point of the implicate order is to turn this approach upside down, and to regard the implicate order as fundamental, while the explicate order is then understood as having unfolded from the implicate order (Bohm and Peat, 1987).

Even in the orthodox Copenhagen interpretation of quantum theory, we have an alternating contraction and dispersion, or unfoldment and enfoldment. For, every time the quantum wave function is "collapsed" (by observation or whatnot) this is its sudden contraction. After that, the wave function again begins to spread or disperse (in "probability space" here, but still propagating via Green's function), until its next collapse/contraction. As such, the existence of that basic, cyclic collapse/dispersion process in quantum theory—and thus of "implicate"/enfolding and "explicate"/unfolding phenomena—is not at all arguable. (Of course, the linear nature of Schrödinger's equation does not actually allow for such discontinuous behavior as would be required in order for its wave-solutions to "collapse" instantaneously [Bohm and Peat, 1987]. That, however, is a separate point/inconsistency in the accepted view.)

> [B]asically all the laws of movement in quantum mechanics do correspond to enfoldment and unfoldment. In particular, the relation between the wave function at one time ... and its form at another [later] time ... is determined by the propagator or the Green's function....
>
> A simple picture of the movement is that waves from the whole space enfold into each region and that waves from each region unfold back into the whole space....
>
> Since all matter is now analyzed in terms of quantum fields, and since the movements of all these fields are expressed in terms of propagators, *it is implied by current physics* that the implicate order is universal (Bohm and Hiley, 1993; italics added).

In any case, the observable motions of particles in both Newtonian and quantum physics are part of the same explicate order. Thus, any attempt to associate quantum physics only with the "more wholistic" implicate order would be woefully misled, as Bohm himself noted:

> Clearly the manifest world of common sense experience refined where necessary with the aid of the concepts and laws of classical physics is basically in an explicate order. But *the motion of particles at the quantum level is evidently also in an explicate order* (Bohm and Hiley, 1993; italics added).

All of that is fundamental and inherent to Bohm's mature formulation of quantum theory, and existed well prior to Wilber's first comments on that in the late '70s.

The explicate order is again a part or a subset of the whole implicate order. That is, the latter implicate order *transcends but includes* the explicate order. Or, as Bohm again explicitly stated in Hiley and Peat (1987), the explicate order is "contained within" the implicate, not merely by analogy but by the mathematics of his ontological formulation. (You cannot get much less "mutually exclusive" than to have one thing *contain another* within itself.) And that inclusion, of course, is exactly what Wilber wants higher levels of reality to do with respect to their juniors, in accord with the theory and theology underlying the perennial philosophy or Great Chain of Being.

So why, then, is kw so unhappy whenever it comes to Bohm's genuinely brilliant ideas, as compared to his own? Wilber could, after all, with minimal "transpersonalizing" of the physics, easily have taken those very concepts as largely *supporting* rather than *competing with* his own, had he wished to properly represent them.

Of course, none of the above would make naïve, transpersonal attempts to map astral-level *prana* (or even the nondual Absolute) to the implicate order, and physical matter to the explicate, any more valid. (It could be said regardless, though, via Bohm's "converging/dispersing water wave" and ink-drop analogies, that the explicate order "condenses out of" the implicate, as matter is believed to do from astral *prana.)* It does, however, demonstrate that Wilber has fundamentally misunderstood and grossly misrepresented Bohm's ideas, here. For again, *nowhere* did Bohm ever "originally explain" that the explicate and implicate orders are mutually exclusive, as kw wrongly claims. Indeed, had Bohm ever done that, he would have been radically misunderstanding the most basic nature of his own Nobel-caliber theories.

Even just in terms of the ink-drop analogy, there are an infinite number of intermediate steps in which the drop is partly implicated, and partly explicated. Thus, it was never a question of the drop being *either* implicated *or* explicated, with those extreme states being forever mutually exclusive, as Wilber dualistically imagines. Even the existence of Bohm's (1980) "implication parameter"—"the number of turns required to bring a given droplet of dye into [fully] explicate form"—would have disclosed as much.

## 2. THE SUPER-IMPLICATE ORDER

Regarding the existence of the super-implicate order, David Bohm, in Weber (1986), has given the following information:

> In talking of a super-implicate order, I am not making any further assumptions beyond what is implied in physics today. Once we extend this ["pilot wave"] model of de Broglie to the quantum mechanical field rather than just to the particle, that picture immediately is the super-implicate order. So this is not speculation, it is the picture which is implied by present quantum mechanics if you look at it imaginatively.

Obviously, that solid basis cannot be reduced to the idea that Bohm might have just been "making up new levels" as he went along, even if the super-implicate order is itself reasonably regarded as being merely part of a still-greater order, to not be "the last word" in that. (The dialog from which the above block quote is drawn was first published in *ReVision* in 1983, at a time when Wilber [1999b] himself *was still editing that journal.*) There is thus precisely nothing "awkward" about the chronological development of Bohm's ideas, in him adding those levels, as he himself explained (in Hiley and Peat, 1987):

> [T]he original [holographic quantum mechanical particle theory] model was one in which the whole was constantly enfolded into and unfolded from each region of an electromagnetic field, through dynamical movement and development of the field according to the laws of classical field theory. But now [i.e., in extending this model to the quantum mechanical field], this whole field is no longer a self-contained totality; it depends crucially on the super-quantum potential. As we have seen, however, this in turn depends on the "wave function of the universe" in a way that is a generalization of how

the quantum potential for particles depends on the wave function of a system of particles. But all such wave functions are forms of the implicate order (whether they refer to particles or to fields). Thus, the super-quantum potential expresses the activity of a new kind of implicate order [i.e., the super-implicate order].

That perspective then incorporates both the idea of the implicate order being a "movement of outgoing and incoming waves," and Bohm's original "causal" (or "hidden variable") interpretation of quantum theory. (The latter formulation was published in 1952, and already contained the quantum potential term.)

The quantum potential appears when one is solving Schrödinger's equation in deriving the "WKB approximation" of quantum theory, for example (see Chapter 3 of Bohm and Hiley [1993]). That (mathematical) term is present immediately alongside the electromagnetic potential acting on the same system. And indeed, the quantum potential, with an effect that does not drop off with increasing distance, exerts a physical force on the matter in its vicinity, just as does the electromagnetic potential. In neither case does matter "arise" from such potentials, nor did the "original meaning" of the quantum potential ever suggest that it might, in spite of Wilber's (1982) misunderstandings to the contrary:

> [M]atter [possibly] arises from a physical energy-sea. This seems to me the original meaning of Bohm's ... quantum potential.

The aforementioned super-implicate order, again, is a field which determines the behavior of the particles of the (first) implicate and the explicate orders. Although it is "the source from which the forms of the first implicate order are generated" (Bohm and Peat, 1987), it is not simply *another* level of enfolding/unfolding particles," akin to another link in the perennial philosophy's Great Chain of Being. (This will become highly relevant later on, regarding Wilber's use of his own misunderstandings in that regard to find additional fault with Bohm's work.)

> The super-implicate order makes the implicate order nonlinear and organizes it into relatively stable forms with complex structures (Bohm, in [Weber, 1986]).

The essential flow [of explicated matter through time] is not
from one place to another but a movement within the implicate and super-implicate ... orders. At every moment, the totality of these orders is present and enfolded throughout all
space so ... they all interpenetrate (Bohm and Peat, 1987).

For the sake of completeness, and because Wilber (1982) has
mentioned its existence, Bohm had this to say about the super-
super-implicate order:

[A] little reflection shows that the whole idea of implicate order could be extended in a natural way. For if there are two
levels of implicate order, why should there not be more?
Thus if we regard the super-implicate order as the second
level, then we might consider a third level which was related
to the second as the second is to the first. That is to say, the
third implicate order would organize the second which would
thereby become non-linear. (For example there might be a
tendency for the whole quantum state to collapse into something more definite) (Bohm and Hiley, 1993).

One would reasonably regard the keeping-open of those possibilities as more of a logical and open-minded position than an
"awkward" one.

Note further that there is no correlation between Bohm's "implication parameter" and the level of implicate order. That is, a
greater degree of dispersion of the ink-drop in the first implicate
order does not equate, even by analogy, to the super-implicate or
higher-level orders. If we were looking for a level which organizes
the implicate order in the ink-drop analogy, one loose option would
be the person turning the handle on the glycerine-filled device.

In any case, the super-implicate order itself, as Bohm explicitly noted, does not require "any further assumptions beyond what
is implied in physics today." That is, contrary to Wilber's misled
claims, it most certainly is "based on empirical findings in physics."

## 3. THE HOLOGRAPHIC NATURE OF (PHYSICAL) REALITY

As Bohm noted in Wilber (1982):

[A]ny form of movement could constitute a hologram, movements known or unknown [i.e., even beyond mere physical

vibrations] and we will consider an undefined totality of movement, called the holomovement and say: the holomovement is the ground of what is manifest.

As such, Bohm's holomovement includes all possible implicate orders, not only his first implicate order.

[T]his enfoldment and unfoldment takes place not only in the movement of the electromagnetic field but also in that of other fields, such as the electronic, protonic, sound waves, etc. There is already a whole host of such fields that are known, and any number of additional ones, as yet unknown, that may be discovered later. Moreover, the movement is only approximated by the classical concept of fields (which is generally used for the explanation of how the hologram works). More accurately, these fields obey quantum-mechanical laws, implying the properties of discontinuity and non-locality (Bohm, 1980).

In no way, then, was the holographic structure of physical reality merely an appealing metaphor grafted onto quantum theory by Bohm.

Even aside from that, the overall idea of there being a holographic nature to reality is most certainly supported by recent physics, in particular in the realm of superstring or M-theory—the physicists' best hope for a "Theory of Everything":

[Dr. Juan] Maldacena's work ... supports a hot new theory that the universe is holographic.... In the Maldacena model, the four-dimensional [quantum] field theory can be thought of as a holographic projection of the five-dimensional string theory (Johnson, 1998).

[I]n certain cases, string theory embodies the holographic principle (Greene, 2000).

Maldacena's work regarding the holographic structure of quantum gravity in superstring theory is by now "a firmly established gravity/gauge theory" (Halbersma, 2002). Between that and Bohm's ideas, then, it would be difficult for anyone to confidently assert that the physical universe is *not* holographic in its structure.

Whenever we are considering the nature of holograms in general, however, the following misunderstanding seems to invariably come up:

> In the hologram, the sum total of the parts is contained in each part (Wilber, 1982).

That idea, however, is not accurate, as Bohm (italics added) explained earlier *in the same book:*

> [I]t is characteristic of the hologram that if you illuminate a part of the hologram you will get the information about the whole picture but *it will be less detailed and from less angles,* so the more of the hologram you take, the more detailed and the more ample the information is always going to be.

Wilber (2003b), too, has recently come to understand that basic principle.

It is therefore incorrect to say that every piece or part of a holographic plate contains *all* (i.e., the "sum total") of the information about the entire scene. Indeed, the need to illuminate the entire hologram in order to get back all of the information enfolded into it follows from elementary laws of wave behavior, regardless of the type of waves (sound, light, etc.) which are being used to create and then display the hologram.

We have thus seen that Wilber's claim that the implicate and explicate orders are mutually exclusive is not at all valid. Also, contrary to kw's assertions, Bohm's super-implicate order was not merely an arbitrary addition to his earlier work. And, we have very good reason to regard reality as having a holographic structure. All of those distinguishing characteristics of Bohm's work, further, are most certainly "based on empirical findings in physics."

## "WIDESPREAD DISREPUTE"

> [O]ver the last decade and a half [Bohm's work] has generally fallen into widespread disrepute (and it has no support whatsoever from recent physics).

We will consider that statement in two parts: first in terms of the evolving reputation of Bohm's ideas, and then with regard to the documented support from recent physics for those same ideas. In doing so, we shall see that Wilber has unabashedly misrepresented the realities of both of those.

## REPUTATION

It is not clear from the ambiguities in Wilber's writing whether the "disrepute" he is attributing to Bohm's ideas refers merely to their relation to fuzzy, transpersonal "holographic paradigms" in general, or to serious physics. If the latter, consider the following:

> Due largely to a 1994 *Scientific American* cover story and F. David Peat's *Infinite Potential—The Life and Times of David Bohm* (1997), the means by which Bohm's alternative quantum theory had been effectively suppressed came to light, and the general outlines of this alternative were finally presented to a substantial reading public. This theory, developed in collaboration with Prof. Basil Hiley and known in its mature form as the "ontological interpretation" of quantum mechanics, is now *widely viewed as a serious critique of the Copenhagen interpretation* [italics added], and proffers a revisioning of quantum theory in which objective reality is restored and undivided wholeness is fundamental (Lee Nichol, in [Bohm, 2003]).

The lack of "objective reality" in the orthodox interpretation was indeed one of Einstein's primary objections to it, even above its "dice-playing," indeterministic nature.

From a more hard-nosed perspective, consider the testimony of skeptic Martin Gardner. (Gardner wrote the "Mathematical Games" column for *Scientific American* for more than twenty-five years, and was largely responsible for bringing knowledge of fractals to the masses via that medium in 1978.) Indeed, Gardner's efforts at debunking New Age ideas have earned him the praise of both Stephen Jay Gould and Noam Chomsky. Yet he had this to say (2000; italics added) about Bohm's ontological formulation of quantum mechanics:

> [T]his theory, long ignored by physicists, is now gaining *increasing* support. It deserves to be better known.

Gardner there is endorsing the quantum potential aspect of Bohm's ideas, not the implicate and explicate orders which Bohm found to exist in the mathematics of both the orthodox formulation and in his own. Nevertheless, as far as support from physicists for Bohm's ideas goes, in Gardner's wholly non-mystical regard that very advocacy is *increasing*.

Likewise, Eric Dennis (2001; italics added) has noted that, contrary to past "almost maniacal" reactions to the "dissidents" in quantum physics, and to Bohm in particular,

> the last *two decades* have brought major changes.... Indeed, there now seems to be *increasing* support among physicists for exorcising the [Copenhagen interpretation-based] notion of observer-created reality from the foundations of physical science.

Of course, if Wilber's asserted "widespread disrepute" of Bohm's ideas was referring simply to the fading hopes of the "holographic paradigm" within transpersonal/integral psychology, he may well be right about the increasing disrepute of that endeavor. For, those attempts by his fellow transpersonal and integral psychologists (not by Bohm) to split psychological stages or states of consciousness between the implicate and explicate orders are indeed not worthy of serious consideration.

Regardless, even widespread "ill repute" (whether in serious physics, transpersonal/integral psychology, or both) would at most show the temporary unpopularity of a theory, not say anything about its truth-value. That is, given a community of intersubjective interpreters who have not bothered to properly understand the theory in the first place, as has been the case with Bohm's ideas in both physics (Peat, 1997) and transpersonal/integral psychology, its degree of repute or disrepute is wholly irrelevant. That, indeed, is even aside from the separate problem that theories and paradigms again do not generally gain acceptance simply via any force of logical persuasion in their arguments. Rather, they eventually become accepted via the "old generation" of intersubjective interpreters dying out.

Having said all that, though, we still cannot help but note that both John S. Bell and Richard Feynman contributed papers, in explicit honor, celebration and good repute of Bohm and his work in serious physics, to Hiley and Peat's (1987) *Quantum Implications*. (Bell was the creator of Bell's Inequality, which he developed on the basis of Bohm's work. Feynman was a Nobel Prize winner, and heir to Einstein's mantle of being regarded as "perhaps the smartest man in the world." He had little interest in the fundamental issues of physics or philosophy, yet considered Bohm to be a "great" physicist [Peat, 1997], deferring to the latter's expositions in their talks together.) So too did Geoffrey Chew, Henry Stapp, Roger Penrose, Ilya Prigogine and David Finkelstein. That (1987) "book of good repute" was, of course, published well within "the last decade and a half" of Wilber's (1998) initial quote, above.

## SUPPORT

In terms of Wilber's suggestion that Bohm's ontological formulation, with its implicate and explicate orders, has "no support whatsoever from recent physics," we can be even more categorical. For, there it is very clear that he is referring to hard science, not to transpersonal/integral psychology's (mis)appropriation of Bohm's ideas.

To begin, we note that the ontological formulation of quantum theory, by the very manner of its derivation, will always be compatible with the orthodox theory. That is, any experimental results which are in harmony with the orthodox theory will also accord with Bohm's reformulation. As such, there is no experiment for which the orthodox theory could be "right," and Bohm's explanations "wrong" (Bohm and Hiley, 1993).

Conversely, any experiment which supports orthodox quantum theory—as every existing one has—will perforce also support Bohm's causal/ontological formulation. Therefore, Bohm's view has just as much support from recent physics in that regard as does the orthodox quantum theory.

Alternatively, if the alleged "absence of support from recent physics" derives from the idea that attempts to unify quantum theory and general relativity via superstring or M-theory have thus far not included the implicate/explicate order concepts, that position need hardly be taken seriously. For, if the theorists working on M-theory are only hoping to integrate the orthodox quantum theory, not Bohm's more-detailed formulation, into that "Theory of Everything," then of course the implicate/explicate order structure will not be openly brought over into it, and thus not mentioned in relevant scholarly or popularized literature. Integrating Bohm's ontological formulation into superstring theory would automatically integrate the orthodox theory—since the ontological formulation mathematically simplifies to the orthodox view—but not vice versa.

In any case, with or without that integration,

> physicists have not as yet been able to make predictions
> [from superstring theory] with the precision necessary to
> confront experimental data....
>
> Nevertheless ... with a bit of luck, one central feature of
> string theory could receive experimental verification within
> the next decade. And with a good deal more luck, indirect
> fingerprints of the theory could be confirmed at any moment
> (Greene, 2000).

Dr. Brian Greene himself is not merely a popularizer of superstring theory, but a professional physicist and significant contribu-
tor to it.

As to the state of recent physics outside of superstring theory,
the Nobel Prize-winner Sheldon Glashow—the "archrival of string
theory through the 1980s"—has admitted (in Greene, 2000) that,
as of 1997,

> non-string theorists [in conventional quantum field theory]
> have not made any progress whatsoever in the last decade.

In terms of looking for "support from recent physics," then, we
evidently have one half of physics which had not progressed in the
decade prior to Wilber's (1998) denigration of Bohm—and thus has
nothing to say about "recent" developments in the field. On the
other hand, the superstring half of the profession has a theory
which may, "with a bit of luck," be testable in *one* aspect of its core
within a decade or so after that denigration!

Clearly, then, there is nothing within the recent developments
in physics to in any way gainsay Bohm's ideas.

And how does orthodox quantum theory fare in the superstring theorists' "recent physics" view?

> [M]any string theorists [who tend to be unfamiliar with the
> details of Bohm's work] foresee a *reformulation* of how quan-
> tum principles are incorporated into our theoretical descrip-
> tion of the universe as the next major upheaval in our under-
> standing (Greene, 2000; italics added).

After all that, we should now consider the relevance of Bohm's
ideas to the deep understanding of fundamental issues in physics:

[D]espite the empirical equivalence between Bohmian mechanics and orthodox quantum theory, there are a variety of experiments and experimental issues that don't fit comfortably within the standard quantum formalism but are easily handled by Bohmian mechanics [i.e., by the ontological formulation of quantum theory]. Among these are dwell and tunneling times, escape times and escape positions, scattering theory, and quantum chaos (Goldstein, 2002).

According to Richard Feynman, the two-slit experiment for electrons [which clearly shows the wave-particle duality inherent in quantum particles] is "a phenomenon which is impossible, *absolutely* impossible, to explain in any classical way, and which has in it the heart of quantum mechanics. In reality it contains the *only* mystery." This experiment "has been designed to contain all of the mystery of quantum mechanics, to put you up against the paradoxes and mysteries and peculiarities of nature one hundred per cent." As to the question, "How does it really work? What machinery is actually producing this thing? Nobody knows any machinery. Nobody can give you a deeper explanation of this phenomenon than I have given; that is, a description of it."

But Bohmian mechanics is just such a deeper explanation (Goldstein, 2002).

Compare Feynman's above presentation, from within the perspective of orthodox quantum theory, with J. S. Bell's (1987; italics added) explanation of the same experimental context, based on Bohm's formulation of quantum mechanics (which originated as an extension of an idea first proposed independently by Louis de Broglie in the late 1920s):

De Broglie showed in detail how the motion of a particle, passing through just one of two holes in screen, could be influenced by waves propagating through both holes. And so influenced that the particle does not go where the waves cancel out, but is attracted to where they cooperate. This idea seems to me so natural and simple, to resolve the wave-particle dilemma in such a clear and ordinary way, that it is a great mystery to me that it was so generally ignored. Of the founding fathers, only *Einstein thought that de Broglie was on the right lines.*

If one is truly interested in understanding what is going on beneath phenomenological appearances in the physical universe, then, one has *no choice* but to give an audience to formulations such as Bohm's. As such, whatever degree of "support" may be given or withheld from Bohm's ideas by "recent physics," his ideas—and the questions as to the basic nature of reality which he courageously and insightfully asked—are absolutely relevant. Without such questioning there is no hope of understanding how the universe really works, in ways beyond the severe ontological limitations of the Copenhagen interpretation (in which one is not allowed to ask "what happens" to reality in between observations of it).

Taking all of that into account, the best that one can say about the assertion (by Wilber) that Bohm's ontological interpretation "has no support whatsoever from recent physics" is that that idea itself is wholly unsupportable.

One might hope that Wilber's perspective on this subject had improved in the twenty-plus years since his original "strong" critique of Bohm. Unfortunately, however, such is not the case, as we can see from his recent (2003) writings. Those are posted online as part of 200,000 words worth of "first draft" excerpts from the forthcoming installments in his "Kosmos" trilogy:

> [T]he simplistic and dualistic notion that there is, for example, an implicate order (which is spiritual and quantum) and an explicate order (which is material and Newtonian) has caused enormous confusion, and is still doing so. But even David Bohm, who introduced that notion, eventually ended up tacking so many epicycles on it that it became unrecognizable....
>
> [I]f you absolutize physics ... then you will collapse the entire Great Chain into merely one implicate and one explicate order....
>
> Bohm vaguely realized this—and realized that his "implicate order," precisely because it was set apart from the explicate order, could not actually represent any sort of genuine or nondual spiritual reality. He therefore invented a third realm, the "super-implicate order," which was supposed to be the nondual spiritual realm. He then had three levels of reality: explicate, implicate, super-implicate. But because he was unfamiliar with the subtleties of Shunyata [i.e., trans-conceptual, metaphysical "Emptiness"] ... he was still caught in dualistic notions (because he was still trying to qualify the

unqualifiable). He therefore added yet another epicycle: "beyond the superimplicate," to give him four levels of reality....

This is not the union of science and spirituality, but the union of bad physics with bad mysticism.

At the risk of being overly repetitive, we again note the following:

- At no point, going back to pre-1980, did Bohm ever regard the implicate order as being "spiritual and quantum," and the explicate order as "material and Newtonian." It is *Wilber* who has misread those orders as being mutually exclusive or "dualistic." For Bohm himself, on the other hand, the explicate order was always a subset of the transcending/including implicate order.

  The localized explicate order is indeed more like the "separate particles" of Newtonian physics, with the diffused implicate order being more like the nonlocal interconnectedness of quantum theory. That fact, however, does not in any way mean that one could ever equate the explicate order with Newtonian physics, or the implicate order with quantum theory.

  By the "correspondence principle" in quantum mechanics, quantum physics must reduce to classical, Newtonian physics, when appropriate limits are taken. Thus, Newtonian physics, too, is a *subset* of quantum theory, not something mutually exclusive to it. Therefore, one could never coherently associate quantum physics with the implicate order, and Newtonian physics with the explicate, while simultaneously claiming that those two orders are mutually exclusive.

  Given Wilber's insistent misconception that the implicate and explicate orders are mutually exclusive, it is no surprise that when he attempts, for purposes of argument, to map degrees of subtly in (e.g., astral) matter, to levels of the implicate order, he cannot do so. If he were to instead map those subtleties, not to levels of implicate and superimplicate order within the totality of such orders, but rather to a literal spectrum of frequencies of consciousness within an implicate/explicate order which is not limited to the realm of physics but includes subtle matter as well (cf. Bentov, 1977), he would find that it works quite nicely.

Of course, whether higher states of consciousness and subtler degrees of matter actually exist, or are mere artifacts of psychoses or of other inabilities to distinguish between reality and one's own fantasies, is a separate question

• Bohm's super-implicate order is fully implied by current physics, as is the implicate order conceptually below it. As such, in no way was the former ever merely an arbitrary, epicycle-like addition for the purpose of correcting inaccuracies in the first level of the implicate order, as Wilber wrongly suggests. The super-implicate order was thus "invented" by Bohm only in a praiseworthy way of discovery, not a derogatory one.

Further, none of those levels of implicate order were ever equated with nondual Spirit in Bohm's view. Rather, Spirit as the highest state of consciousness (and immanent ground of all lower states) was always beyond (but suffusing) all levels of the (relatively unmanifest, but not transcendent Unmanifest) implicate order:

> Obviously, the nonmanifest that we talk about [i.e., the hierarchy of implicate orders] is a relative nonmanifest. It is still a thing, although a subtle thing .... [W]hatever we would mean by what is beyond matter [e.g., Spirit] we cannot grasp in thought....
>
> However subtle matter becomes, it is not true [G]round of all [B]eing (Bohm, in [Wilber, 1982]).

Note again that the above statement comes from the *very same book* which Wilber both edited and re-printed his own initial "strong criticism" of Bohm in.

Bohm reasonably included consciousness, thought and emotion within his own view of "matter" (of varying degrees of subtlety), and as such placed them all within the implicate order(s). Nondual Spirit, however, was always something beyond all such qualifiable orders, in his view. That is, it was never merely the highest of Bohm's implicate orders, even if he occasionally spoke of those implicate orders "shading off" into Unqualifiable Spirit

• Wilber's suggestion that Bohm's development of gradations or levels in the implicate order had anything to do with Bohm trying to "qualify the unqualifiable" is wholly without validity. More specifically, the notion that Bohm's ideas arose from him being "unfamiliar with the subtleties of Shunyata" is completely misplaced. Rather, Bohm's understanding of the limitations of human "dualistic" thought was every bit as sophisticated as is Wilber's:

> [Y]ou may try to get a view of [S]pirit as the notion of God as immanent. But both immanent [i.e., Spirit-as-Ground] and transcendent God [Spirit-as-Source] would have to be *beyond thought* [and thus beyond mathematical expression in any implicate order] (Bohm, in [Wilber, 1982]—again, *the very same book* containing Wilber's original critique—italics added)

- As far as Bohm's brilliant ideas being "bad physics" goes, we have already seen that numerous top-flight physicists (among them Richard Feynman, J. S. Bell and Ilya Prigogine), have given a more informed view. Their endorsements of Bohm's ideas, versus Wilber's disparaging of the same, further have absolutely nothing to do with Wilber possessing a nondual One Taste realization or even an intellectual understanding of spirituality which they might lack. Rather, those individuals are simply professionals who understand physics at a level which Wilber clearly does not. They are thus able to recognize groundbreaking, sensible ideas in that field when they see them. One may indeed rest fully assured that neither Feynman nor Bell nor Prigogine would have respected Bohm's ontological formulation of quantum mechanics, had that theory been full of arbitrary, epicycle-like ideas

- When Bohm says that "the holomovement is the ground of what is manifest" (in Wilber, 1982), he is not identifying it with the (mathematically inexpressible) immanent Ground or Suchness of the perennial philosophy. Rather, he is simply viewing that movement as containing everything within manifestation

- Wilber himself has gone through numerous phases in his thought, which are by now widely known as Wilber-1 through Wilber-4, with Wilber-5 already on the way.

> Bohm's thought, too, advanced through comparable stages,
> even though it has never been categorized as "Bohm-1,"
> etc. Wilber-2 was not merely a derogatory "epicycle" tacked
> onto Wilber-1, and so on (though his grafted-on lines of de-
> velopment are close to being exactly that). The same toler-
> ance should obviously apply to one's view of the sequential
> development of Bohm's levels of implicate order

Wilber's improvements to his model of consciousness are (purportedly) grounded in empirical research in psychology. Bohm's
levels of implicate order, likewise, are certainly based on empirical
research in physics. Indeed, they are grounded in measurement to
a *far* greater degree of precision than one will find in any of Wilber's own work, or for that matter in anything extant in transpersonal psychology or integral studies.

Bohm is thus guilty of neither "bad physics" nor of "bad mysticism." Wilber, however, is embarrassingly culpable, if not for both
of those, then for the worse repeated violence against a mere
"straw man" misrepresentation, created by no one but himself, of
Bohm's ideas.

Amazingly, none of the points discussed here require an advanced understanding of physics or mathematics in order for one
to sort fact from fiction. Rather, all that they ever required was for
one to read Bohm's self-popularized ideas carefully, and thus to
properly understand them.

Note further that, through all of this, no "interpretation" of
Bohm's ideas is involved. Rather, all that one has to do is to look at
what Bohm actually said in print, and compare that with Wilber's
presentation of the same ideas—often in the same (1982) book, no
less—to see the glaring distortions in the latter.

In writing this defense, I have been given pause to wonder
why Bohm himself never responded to Wilber's original (and relatively well-tempered, compared to the gratuitous unkindness in
[1998] and [2003]) critique. For, nearly everything quoted throughout this paper was already present in Bohm's own published writings. Indeed, anything which wasn't already in print two decades
ago could easily have been produced by him in writing "over a
weekend."

Bohm of course passed away in 1992, after having suffered
aperiodic crippling depressions throughout his life, notably in the

final decade of that. Yet through all that, he continued working on his own thrillingly original ideas in both physics and metaphysics.

The answer most likely lies in Bohm's overall attitude toward productive dialog—applied just as well in his interactions with professional physicists. Earlier in his life, arguments between Bohm and his colleagues would occasionally escalate to shouting, heard all the way down the corridors from his office. After one particularly belligerent public confrontation, however, in a realization that he and his opponent were not communicating, Bohm ceased that adversarial way of working (Peat, 1997).

Also, as time wore on, Bohm's ideas drifted ever-farther from the mainstream in both physics and metaphysics. He thus predictably encountered the additional problem of finding it extremely rare for him to meet anyone with the open-mindedness and background necessary for them to have a productive conversation. Rather, he would have first needed to spend several days explaining his entire philosophy and metaphysics, before any satisfying communication could occur.

One might then very reasonably relate Bohm's non-responsiveness to Wilber's demonstrated misunderstandings and distinctly inadequate background in physics to these same ideas, and indeed could do so almost point by point. Bohm would, after all, have had to write (if not talk) for at least several days, in explaining how Wilber had misunderstood his work. And in doing so, unlike other writing in which he passionately indulged, Bohm would have discovered few if any new ideas for himself. Instead, that time would have necessarily been spent just re-hashing what he had already explicitly and implicitly put into print, and which was thus already available for anyone who cared to read his books and interviews with even a minimally attentive eye.

In any case, as far as the lack of response to Wilber's critiques over the decade since Bohm's death goes, few of Bohm's admirers, past or present, have had a background in both physics and metaphysics. And overall, such a background is necessary in order for one to understand Bohm's ideas well enough to realize how drastically Wilber has misrepresented them.

For the present purposes, as we have seen, all that one has to do in order to see the relevant misrepresentations of Bohm's work by Wilber is to "A-B" Bohm versus Wilber. In doing so, one will again readily recognize that where Bohm himself explicitly calls something "white," Wilber is claiming that Bohm has called it "black," and then deriding him for that, from no more than a straw-man perspective of Bohm's work, which Wilber himself has solely created.

If there is one overarching point which we can take from all that, then, it would be that ideas which have been proved "wrong" and "impossible" by seemingly watertight logical argument today may well be shown to be not merely possible but unavoidable tomorrow. Conversely, arguing so persuasively in favor of wrong or grossly misrepresented ideas that they seem to be inarguably correct can easily do more harm than good in the service of truth. In such a case, merely "doing one's best" to spread one's preferred gospel, whether integral or otherwise, is in no way good enough.

At any rate, a "late" answer to a critique is better than none at all; and the interim absence of the same should never have been confidently taken as a sign that the bold misrepresentations of Bohm's brilliant and precise work, on Wilber's unapologetic and inexcusably sloppy part, were unanswerable.

As Robert Carroll (2003) has noted, Wilber's facile arguments against Darwinian evolution "dismiss one of the greatest scientific ideas ever in a few paragraphs" of what can only charitably be called gross misrepresentations. And having gotten away with that sleight-of-mind, kw *does exactly the same thing to **another*** of the truly "greatest scientific ideas" ever—in Bohm's Nobel-caliber reformulation of quantum mechanics—in a comparable number of indefensibly misrepresentative paragraphs.

Interestingly, Albert Einstein himself—a man not prone to endorsing epicycles or "simplistic notions"—considered David Bohm to be his "intellectual successor" and "intellectual son" (Peat, 1997):

> It was Einstein who had said, referring to the need for a radical new quantum theory, "if anyone can do it, then it will be Bohm."

Conversely, Bohm did not "realize the indefensible nature of his position"—there was no "indefensible nature" to realize, only a Nobel-caliber one.

Perhaps significantly, practically nowhere does Wilber ever quote directly from (or provide page references for) the work he is claiming to synthesize or critique. Instead, he throws out long lists of scholars whose work ostensibly supports whatever point he may be trying to make at the time. As a writing style for popularizing established ideas, that would be one thing. And even when one is attempting to bring hundreds of different psychological models into a coherent spectrum, it may be partly understandable. For, the man's books have never tended toward the slim side, even with that relatively concise approach.

Still, that method puts readers in the precarious position of having to either trust kw to have properly represented other people's ideas—which the overwhelming majority of his admirers would indeed be fully willing to do—or find the time to reproduce the mounds of research themselves. In doing the latter, though, they would be pitting themselves against an "Einstein" who *would surely not have gotten to that high position of respect were his work not all that it is claimed to be.*

Ironically, Wilber himself has suffered much misrepresentation of his work by others. Indeed, in the midst of his claims that he greatly values "responsible criticism," he has opined:

> [Often] somebody will give a blistering attack on, say, Wilber-2, and that attack gets repeated by others who are *trying to nudge me out of the picture* (Wilber, 2001c; italics added).

KW goes on to assert, probably reasonably, that misrepresentation of his work is present in over 80% of the published/posted criticisms of it.

Bohm's work too, however, again involved a chronological development of the ideas (or Bohm-1, Bohm-2), etc. When Wilber criticizes Bohm for his own wrong perceptions in seeing tacked-on "epicycles" in the latter's work, then, he is doing very nearly exactly what he rightly will not accept in argument from his own critics.

One might conclude, then, by parity of argument, that in behaving thusly Wilber is trying to nudge *Bohm* "out of the picture," even without being consciously aware of that.

Likewise, Wilber (2001c) quotes Keith Thompson to the effect that, given the various "studied" misrepresentations of kw's work, none of which involved mere differences of interpretation, it becomes difficult to not attribute "bad faith" to Wilber's critics.

By parity of argument, though, one must then allow for equal "bad faith" on the part of Wilber himself, in his studied misrepresentations of Bohm's ideas. For none of those, too, can be reduced to differences of interpretation.

Further, contrary to Wilber's claim that he "greatly appreciate[s] responsible criticism," he has (to my knowledge) totally ignored Lane's (1996) solid deconstruction of the numerous invalid aspects of his worldview. By contrast, he did find time to respond (1999) in excruciating detail to Heron's (1997) more recent critique of his psychological model, and even later to Hans-Willi Weis (Wilber, 2003a) and de Quincey (Wilber, 2001c). Of course, those responses were given in contexts where, unlike the situation with Lane, Wilber could show, at least to his own satisfaction, that the criticisms of his ideas were not valid. (Needless to say, more recently, kw has given no satisfactory response to Meyerhoff's excellent work—containing research and reasoning *far* superior to his own, by any scholarly evaluation. Nor has he, to my knowledge, even admitted to being aware of the previous online publication of any of the components of the present book.)

And note: Lane actually endorsed Wilber's (1983b) *A Sociable God,* saying that it was "not only destined to become a classic, but also adds further testimony to the fact that Wilber may single-handedly alter the course of future research in consciousness." That is, Lane—like myself—began as an admirer of Wilber, but just kept thinking and researching. And that is all that anyone actually needs to do, to extricate himself from Wilber's slanted version of reality. That, though, is also why the transpersonal and integral communities will ever fail to competently police themselves: people who keep reading outside of the field, into skeptical perspectives, predictably soon leave the discipline. All that is left, then, are the ones who cannot do competent research to save their lives, or otherwise face the basic facts of reality.

In defending his own published polemics, Wilber (2000) has offered the following misleading explanations:

> *Sex, Ecology, Spirituality* is in some ways an angry book. Anger, or perhaps anguish, it's hard to say which. After three years immersed in postmodern cultural studies, where the common tone of discourse is rancorous, mean-spirited, arrogant, and aggressive ... after all of that, in anger and anguish, I wrote SES, and the tone of the book indelibly reflects that.
>
> In many cases it is specific: I often mimicked the tone of the critic I was criticizing, matching toxic with toxic and

snide with snide. Of course, in doing so I failed to turn the other cheek. But then, there are times to turn the other cheek, and there are times not to.

As for the dozen or so theorists that I polemically criticized [in the first edition of *Sex, Ecology, Spirituality*], every single one of them, *without exception,* had engaged in "condemnatory rhetoric" of equal or usually much worse dimensions (Wilber, 2001c; italics added).

Bohm, however, although not mentioned in SES—except in that his (1980) *Wholeness and the Implicate Order* is included in the bibliography, though once again being mis-dated there as 1973 —*is* an exception to that self-absolution. For, he never stooped to any such nasty, snide behavior toward Wilber. Thus, the above rationalizations cannot be validly applied to justifying kw's unduly vexed comments about Bohm's consistently honest, humble and insightful work. The most that Bohm was ever "guilty" of was in having simply never responded to Wilber's original (1982), off-base but relatively well-tempered critique, nothing more provocative.

What are the odds, then, that Wilber's polemics in other contexts can be excused as being altogether noble attempts to "spiritually awaken" others? Or as having arisen only from others having "started" the mud-slinging? A betting man would not, one supposes, wager in favor of that.

Conversely, what are the far better odds that he is simply not being psychologically honest with himself as to the basis of his anger, cloaking it instead in a veneer of high ideals?

In further defending his behavior toward others, Wilber (1999) has written:

Even in my most polemical statements, they are always balanced, if you look at all of my writing, by an appreciation of the positive contributions of those I criticize.

Sadly, that claim, too, is untrue. For, in no way did Wilber provide any such balance himself in his own (1998 and 2003) attempted demolitions of Bohm, or anywhere else throughout his life's work. It is difficult, after all, to "appreciate" what you have not understood—as Wilber proves in his original (1982) critique. That is so, particularly if the potential validity of the competing ideas seems to threaten your own high place in the world.

Wilber may have feebly *tried* to "appreciate" Bohm's work there, but he certainly did not succeed, instead at best misrepresenting and damning it with *very* faint praise relative to its Nobel caliber.

Wilber (2001c) then poses the rhetorical question as to his own motivations for lashing out at others:

> Did they do anything to possibly bring it on themselves, or was this just a unilateral case of me being rotten to the core?

In the case of his dissing of Bohm, however, it absolutely *was* demonstrably a "unilateral case" of Wilber "being rotten to the core." For, Bohm never provoked Wilber in any way, except by being right (and silent, even while alive; and moreso since then) where Wilber has been embarrassingly, confidently and verbosely wrong. (Throughout the 1980s, Bohm was a near guru-figure to the "holographic" New Age movement—a position obviously coveted intensely by Wilber, and reason enough for him to do all he could to discredit his primary "competitor.")

Significantly, following his (1998) misrepresentations of Bohm's work, and even while utterly failing to respond to Lane's (1996) devastating deconstruction of his foibles, Wilber himself again expressed the following confident opinion:

> Until this ["straw man," in kw's case] critique is even vaguely answered, I believe we must consider Bohm's theory to be refuted.

By parity of argument, then, until Wilber has even vaguely answered *this* critique....

Note: I submitted (and received confirmation of receipt for) an earlier version of this paper to *The Journal of Transpersonal Psychology*, for peer review, in November of 2003. That process "generally takes 6+ months." As of February, 2009, I have yet to receive a verdict from them as to whether properly researched and coherent ideas such as these have a place among their other "make believe" theorizings. Nor am I optimistic about that status changing.

No surprise, then, that there are so few published criticisms of Wilber's work, if that is what happens to even the most thorough of them.

# BIBLIOGRAPHY

Adherents (2005 [2001]), "Composite U.S. Demographics" (http://www.adherents.com/adh_dem.html).

Alexander, Charles and Ellen Langer, ed. (1990), *Higher Stages of Human Development* (New York: Oxford University Press).

American Atheists (2006), "The Ultimate Outsiders? New Report Casts Atheists as 'Others' Beyond Morality and Community in America" (http://www.atheists.org/flash.line/ath1.htm).

Andrews, Jim (2005a), "Twenty *Boomeritis* Blunders: Shoddy Scholarship, Salacious Sex, and Sham Spirituality" (http://www.strippingthegurus.com/stgsamplechapters/twentyboomeritisblunders.asp).

Andrews, Jim (2005), "Ken Wilber on Meditation: A Baffling Babbling of Unending Nonsense" (http://www.strippingthegurus.com/stgsamplechapters/kenwilberonmeditation.asp).

Anthony, Dick, Bruce Ecker and Ken Wilber (1987), *Spiritual Choices: The Problem of Recognizing Authentic Paths to Inner Transformation* (New York: Paragon House).

Aurobindo, Sri (1953), *Sri Aurobindo on Himself and on the Mother* (Pondicherry, India: Sri Aurobindo Ashram).

Austin, Bill (1999), "Rev. Thomas Alhburn, Writer of
Endorsements, Finally Meets Da"
(http://lightmind.com/thevoid/daism/alhburn-leela.html).

Bailey, David and Faye Bailey (2003), "The Findings"
(http://web.archive.org/web/20031214164954/http://
www.npi-news.dk/page152.htm).

Bauwens, Michel (2006a), "Ken Wilber is Losing It"
(http://blog.p2pfoundation.net/?p=244).

Bauwens, Michel (2006), "On the Logic of Cultism at the Integral
Institutes" (http://blog.p2pfoundation.net/?p=245).

Bauwens, Michel (2004), *Pluralities/Integration,* Issue 15, June 1.
(http://www.kheper.net/topics/Wilber/Cult_of_Ken_Wilber.html).

Beck, Don and Christopher Cowan (2005 [1996]), *Spiral Dynamics:
Mastering Values, Leadership and Change* (Oxford: Blackwell
Publishing, Inc.).

Bell, John S. (1987), *Speakable and Unspeakable in Quantum
Mechanics* (Cambridge: Cambridge University Press).

Bennis, Warren G. and Robert J. Thomas (2002), *Geeks and
Geezers: How Era, Values, and Defining Moments Shape Leaders*
(Boston, MA: Harvard Business School Press).

Berreby, David (2005), *Us And Them: Understanding Your Tribal
Mind* (New York: Little, Brown and Company).

Bentov, Itzhak (1977), *Stalking the Wild Pendulum: On the
Mechanics of Consciousness* (Rochester, VT: Destiny Books).

Bharati, Agehananda (1976), *The Light at the Center* (Santa
Barbara, CA: Ross-Erikson).

Blackmore, Susan (1991), "Is Meditation Good for You?" in *New
Scientist,* July 6
(http://www.newscientist.com/article.ns?id=mg13117765.300).

Bob, Sri (2000), *The Knee of Daism: Deconstructing Adi Da*
(http://lightmind.com/Impermanence/Library/knee/).

Bohm, David (2003), *The Essential David Bohm* (New York: Routledge).

Bohm, David (1980), *Wholeness and the Implicate Order* (New York: Routledge).

Bohm, David (1973), "Quantum Theory as an Indication of a New Order in Physics—Implicate and Explicate Order in Physical Law," in *Physics* (GB), 3.2, June.

Bohm, David and Basil J. Hiley (1993), *The Undivided Universe* (New York: Routledge).

Bohm, David and F. David Peat (1987), *Science, Order, and Creativity* (New York: Bantam Books).

Bonder, Saniel (2003), "Waking Down in Mutuality" (http://www.wakingdown.org).

Bonder, Saniel (1990), *The Divine Emergence of the World-Teacher* (Clearlake, CA: The Dawn Horse Press).

Boucher, Tim (2005), "An Integral Approach to Conspiracy Theory" (http://www.timboucher.com/journal/2005/07/24/an-integral-approach-to-conspiracy-theory/).

Branden, Nathaniel (1999), *The Art of Living Consciously: The Power of Awareness to Transform Everyday Life* (New York: Fireside).

Braun, Kirk (1984), *Rajneeshpuram: The Unwelcome Society—"Cultures Collide in a Quest for Utopia"* (Medford, OR: Scout Creek Press).

Brennan, Barbara Ann (1993), *Light Emerging: The Journey of Personal Healing* (Toronto: Bantam Books).

Brennan, Barbara Ann (1987), *Hands of Light: A Guide to Healing Through the Human Energy Field* (Toronto: Bantam Books).

Brent, Peter (1972), *Godmen of India* (London: Allen Lane).

Brundage, Sandy (2002), "Bad Vibes. Warning: Meditating May Be Hazardous to Your Health," in *SF Weekly,* August 28 (http://www.sfweekly.com/issues/2002-08-28/bayview.html).

Butterfield, Stephen T. (1994), *The Double Mirror: A Skeptical Journey into Buddhist Tantra* (Berkeley, CA: North Atlantic Books).

Carroll, Robert T. (2005d), "Ganzfeld," in *The Skeptic's Dictionary* (http://skepdic.com/ganzfeld.html).

Carroll, Robert T. (2005c), "Penile Plethysmograph (PPG)," in *The Skeptic's Dictionary* (http://skepdic.com/penilep.html).

Carroll, Robert T. (2005b), "Immanuel Velikovsky's *Worlds in Collision*," in *The Skeptic's Dictionary* (http://skepdic.com/velikov.html).

Carroll, Robert T. (2005a), "The Princeton Engineering Anomalies Research (PEAR)," in *The Skeptic's Dictionary* (http://skepdic.com/pear.html).

Carroll, Robert T. (2005), "Gary Schwartz's Subjective Evaluation of Mediums: *Veritas* or Wishful Thinking?" in *The Skeptic's Dictionary* (http://www.skepdic.com/essays/gsandsv.html).

Carroll, Robert T. (2004), "Alien Abduction," in *The Skeptic's Dictionary* (http://www.skepdic.com/aliens.html).

Carroll, Robert T. (2003), "The Skeptic's Dictionary Newsletter 38" (http://www.skepdic.com/news/newsletter38.html).

Carroll, Robert T. (1996), "Dogon and Sirius II," in *The Skeptic's Dictionary* (http://skepdic.com/comments/dogoncom.html).

Carruthers, Peter, Stephen Laurence and Stephen Stich, ed. (2005), *The Innate Mind: Structure And Contents* (New York: Oxford University Press).

Chamberlain, Jim (2006a), "'Sorry, It's Just Over Your Head': Wilber's Response to Recent Criticism" (http://www.integralworld.net/overyourhead.html).

Chamberlain, Jim (2006), "Ken Wilber on Evolution: A Few Comments" (http://www.integralworld.net/chamberlain2.html).

Chopra, Deepak (2000), *How to Know God: The Soul's Journey into the Mystery of Mysteries* (New York: Harmony Books).

Chopra, Deepak and Robert Thurman (2000), *The Path to Enlightenment: Insights into Buddhism* (Carlsbad, CA: Hay House Audio Books).

Chopra, Deepak and Robert Thurman (1999), *God and Buddha—A Dialogue* (Montauk, NY: Mystic Fire Video).

Clinton, Bill (2006), Address at the World Economic Forum (http://gaia.unit.net/wef/worldeconomicforum_annualmeeting2006/default.aspx?sn=17195).

Cohen, Andrew (2002), *Living Enlightenment* (Lenox, MA: Moksha Foundation).

Cohen, Andrew (1992), *Autobiography of an Awakening* (Corte Madera, CA: Moksha Foundation).

Colin, Molly, Peter Seidman and Tony Lewis (1985), "Defectors Voice Several Charges," in *Mill Valley Record,* April 3 (http://www.rickross.com/reference/adida/adida19.html).

Columbia Encyclopedia (2005), "Cannibalism" (http://www.bartleby.com/65/ca/cannibal.html).

Cowan, Christopher (2006), in Sam Rose's "P2P (Peer to Peer) and E-C Theory" (http://humergence.typepad.com/the_never_ending_quest/).

Cowan, Christopher (2005a), "Response to Ken Wilber's Response to 'The Missing Links' of Spiral Dynamics and Ken Wilber, a Posting by Bill Moyer on the Post-Conventional Politics (Post-Con Pol) Discussion List" (http://www.spiraldynamics.org/learning/response_to_wilber.htm).

Cowan, Christopher (2005), "What Do You Think About Writer Ken Wilber's Representation of SD and Graves?" (http://www .spiraldynamics.org/learning/faq/integral.html#Wilber).

Cowan, Christopher (2002), *"Boomeritis* or Bust..." (http://www.spiraldynamics.org/reviews/boomeritis_or_bust.html).

Da, Adi (1995), *The Knee of Listening: The Early-Life Ordeal and the Radical Spiritual Realization of the Divine World-Teacher* (Middletown, CA: The Dawn Horse Press).

Dace, Ted (2005), "The False Dilemma Between Neo-Darwinism and Intelligent Design" (http://www.skepticalinvestigations.org/ controversies/Dace_evolution.htm).

Dallman, Matthew (2006), "Ken Wilber," June 8 (http://www.matthewdallman.com/2006/06/ken-wilber.html).

Dallman, Matthew (2005b), "Ken Wilber on Himself," April 20 (http://www.matthewdallman.com/2005/04/ken-wilber-on-himself.html).

Dallman, Matthew (2005a), "Let Me Set the Record Straight," December 6 (http://www.matthewdallman.com/2005/12/let-me-set-record-straight.html).

Dallman, Matthew (2005), "Group Think and Accountability," March 18 (http://www.matthewdallman.com/2005/03/group-think-and-accountability.html).

Darwin, Charles (1962 [1859]), *The Origin of Species* (London: Collier-MacMillan, Ltd.).

Davis, Stuart (1998), "16 Nudes" (http://www.dreamusher.com/16nudes.html#universecommunion).

Dawkins, Richard (2008 [2006]), *The God Delusion* (New York: Mariner Books).

Dawkins, Richard (1986), *The Blind Watchmaker: Why the Evidence of Evolution Reveals a Universe Without Design* (New York: W. W. Norton & Company).

De Quincey, Christian (2001), "Critics Do. Critics Don't:
A Response to Ken Wilber"
(http://deepspirit.com/sys-tmpl/replytowilber).

De Quincey, Christian (2000), "The Promise of Integralism: A
Critical Appreciation of Ken Wilber's Integral Psychology"
(http://www.deepspirit.com/sys-tmpl/thepromiseofintegralism/).

Dennis, Eric (2001), "Quantum Mechanics and Dissidents," in
*Objective Science,* April
(http://objectivescience.com/articles/ed1_quantum_dissidents.htm).

Desilet, Gregory (2007), "Misunderstanding Derrida and
Postmodernism: Ken Wilber and 'Post-Metaphysics' Integral
Spirituality" (http://www.integralworld.net/desilet.html).

Deval, Jacqueline (2008 [2003]), *Publicize Your Book! An Insider's
Guide to Getting Your Book the Attention It Deserves* (New York:
Perigee).

Dutch, Steven (2001), "Velikovsky"
(http://www.uwgb.edu/dutchs/pseudosc/vlkovsky.htm).

Edis, Taner (2001), "Darwin in Mind: 'Intelligent Design' Meets
Artificial Intelligence," in *Skeptical Inquirer,* Volume 25, No. 2,
March/April
(http://www.csicop.org/si/2001-03/intelligent-design.html).

Edwards, Mark (2006), "Parallel Theories of an AQAL Approach to
Relationality. Part 2. Altitude, Perspectives, and Integral Math"
(http://in.integralinstitute.org/talk.aspx?id=630).

Elias (2000), "The New Pattern"
(http://lightmind.com/thevoid/daismreport-04.html).

Encyclopedia Britannica (2005), "Cannibalism"
(http://www.britannica.com/ebc/article-
9359674?query=cannibalism&ct=).

Falk, Geoffrey (2009 [2005]), *Stripping the Gurus: Sex, Violence,
Abuse and Enlightenment* (Toronto: Million Monkeys Press).

Falk, Geoffrey (2007a), "The Age of Wilberius: Facts and Reality vs. Ken Wilber's 'Integral Age.'"

Falk, Geoffrey (2004), *The Science of the Soul: On Consciousness and the Structure of Reality* (Nevada City, CA: Blue Dolphin Publishing).

Feuerstein, Georg (1992), *Holy Madness* (New York: Arkana).

Feynman, Richard (1989 [1985]), *"Surely You're Joking, Mr. Feynman!": Adventures of a Curious Character* (New York: Bantam).

Fredericks, Anthony D. (2000), *Cannibal Animals: Animals That Eat Their Own Kind* (London: Franklin Watts).

Gardner, Martin (2000), *Did Adam and Eve Have Navels? Discourses on Reflexology, Numerology, Urine Therapy, and Other Dubious Subjects* (New York: W. W. Norton & Company).

Gardner, Martin (1995), "Notes of a Fringe-Watcher," in *Skeptical Inquirer,* Volume 19, No. 3, May/June (http://www.csicop.org/si/9505/tm.html).

Gardner, Martin (1978), "White and Brown Music, Fractal Curves and One-Over-f Fluctuations," in *Scientific American,* April.

Goethean (2006), "Talk:Ken Wilber" (http://en.wikipedia.org/wiki/Talk:Ken_Wilber).

Goethean (2005), "Goethea: An Online Notebook," June 3 (http://goethean.blogspot.com/2005_06_01_goethean_archive.html#111782175639934087).

Goldstein, Sheldon [Shelly] (2002), "Bohmian Mechanics," in *The Stanford Encyclopedia of Philosophy,* Winter (http://plato.stanford.edu/archives/win2002/entries/qm-bohm/).

Goodall, Jane (1979), "Life and Death at Gombe," in *National Geographic,* May.

Gordon, James (1987), *The Golden Guru: The Strange Journey of Bhagwan Shree Rajneesh* (Lexington, MA: The Stephen Greene Press).

Gottfredson, Linda S. (1998), "The General Intelligence Factor," in *Scientific American Presents,* Winter (http://www.psych.utoronto.ca/users/reingold/courses/intelligence/cache/1198gottfred.html).

Greene, Brian (2000 [1999]), *The Elegant Universe: Superstrings, Hidden Dimensions, and the Quest for the Ultimate Theory* (New York: Vintage).

Greenpeace (2003), "Saddam Huggers?" February 10 (http://www.greenpeace.org/international/news/saddam-huggers).

Halbersma, Rein (2002), *Geometry of Strings and Branes* (http://www.ub.rug.nl/eldoc/dis/science/r.s.halbersma).

Hargens, Sean (2001), "Intersubjective Musings: A Response to Christian de Quincey's 'The Promise of Integralism'" (http://wilber.shambhala.com/html/watch/042301_intro.cfm).

Harris, Sam (2004), *The End of Faith* (New York: W. W. Norton & Company, Inc.)

Hassan, Steven (1990 [1988]), *Combatting Cult Mind Control* (Rochester, VT: Park Street Press).

Haugland, Jan (2004), "But what good is half a wing? - The Evolution of Flight" (http://blogs.salon.com/0001561/stories/2003/06/27/butWhatGoodIsHalfAWingTheEvolutionOfFlight.html).

Hemsell, Rod (2002), "Ken Wilber and Sri Aurobindo: A Critical Perspective" (http://www.infinityfoundation.com/mandala/i_es/i_es_hemse_wilber.htm).

Heron, John (1997), "A Way Out for Wilberians" (http://www.integralworld.net/WilbErrs.htm).

Hiley, Basil and F. David Peat (1987), *Quantum Implications: Essays in Honour of David Bohm* (New York: Routledge).

Horgan, John (2003a), *Rational Mysticism: Dispatches from the Border Between Science and Spirituality* (New York: Houghton Mifflin Company).

Horgan, John (2003), "The Myth of the Totally Enlightened Guru" (http://www.johnhorgan.org/work21.htm).

Huston, Tom (2005), "Calling All Spiriteers...," in *What Is Enlightenment?* Issue 28 (http://www.wie.org/j28/spiriteers.asp).

Hyman, Ray (2003), "How Not to Test Mediums: Critiquing the Afterlife Experiments," in *Skeptical Inquirer,* Volume 27, No. 1, January/February (http://www.csicop.org/si/2003-01/medium.html).

Integral (2004), "History" (http://web.archive.org/web/20041011034858/http://www.integralinstitute.org/history.htm).

IntegralNaked (2004), "Who is Ken Wilber?" (http://www.integralnaked.org/contributor.aspx?id=1).

Integrative Spirituality (2007), "The Board of Directors" (http://www.integrativespirituality.org/postnuke/html/modules.php?op=modload&name=Sections&file=index&req=viewarticle&artid=378&page=1).

John, Bubba Free (1974), *Garbage and the Goddess: The Last Miracles and Final Spiritual Instructions of Bubba Free John* (Lower Lake, CA: The Dawn Horse Press).

John, Da Free (1985), *The Dawn Horse Testament* (Middletown, CA: The Dawn Horse Press). Foreword at http://www.beezone.com/Wilber/ken_wilbur_praise.html.

John, Da Free (1980), *Scientific Proof of the Existence of God Will Soon Be Announced by the White House!* (Middletown, CA: The Dawn Horse Press). Foreword at http://www.beezone.com/Wilber/onherocults.html.

Johnson, George (1998), "Almost in Awe, Physicists Ponder 'Ultimate' Theory," in the *New York Times,* September 22.

Kazlev, Alan (2004), "Ken Wilber and Sri Aurobindo"
(http://www.kheper.net/topics/Wilber/Wilber_on_Aurobindo.html).

Kazlev, Alan (2003), "Ken Wilber and Adi Da"
(http://www.kheper.net/topics/Wilber/Da.html).

Klass, Philip J. (2000), "The New Bogus Majestic-12 Documents,"
in *Skeptical Inquirer,* Volume 24, No. 3, May/June
(http://www.csicop.org/si/2000-05/majestic-12.html).

Kramer, Joel and Diane Alstad (1993), *The Guru Papers: Masks of
Authoritarian Power* (Berkeley, CA: Frog, Ltd.).

Kurzweil, Ray (2000 [1999]), *The Age of Spiritual Machines: When
Computers Exceed Human Intelligence* (New York: Penguin Books).

Lane, David Christopher (1996a), "The Paradox of Da Free John"
(http://vm.mtsac.edu/~dlane/datext.html).

Lane, David Christopher (1996), "Critique of Ken Wilber"
(http://elearn.mtsac.edu/dlane/kendebates.htm, also posted with
greater usability at
http://www.geoffreyfalk.com/books/LaneMenu.asp).

Lane, David Christopher and Scott Lowe (1996), *Da: The Strange
Case of Franklin Jones* (http://vm.mtsac.edu/~dlane/dabook.html).

Layton, Deborah (1998), *Seductive Poison: A Jonestown Survivor's
Story of Life and Death in the Peoples Temple* (New York: Anchor
Books).

Lifton, Robert J. (2003), "American Apocalypse," in *The Nation,*
December 22.

Loevinger, Jane (1985), "Ego Development in College," in the
*Journal of Personality and Social Psychology,* Volume 48 (4), 947-
62.

Lowe, Scott (1996), "The Strange Case of Franklin Jones"
(http://www.american-buddha.com/franklin.jones.htm).

MacDougall, Curtis D. (1983), *Superstition and the Press* (Albany,
NY: Prometheus Books).

Matsakis, Aphrodite (1996), *I Can't Get Over It: A Handbook for Trauma Survivors* (Oakland, CA: New Harbinger Publications, Inc.).

Meyerhoff, Jeff (2006d), "Dismissal Vs. Debate: A Reply to Ken Wilber's Audio Rebuttal" (http://www.integralworld.net/meyerhoff6.html).

Meyerhoff, Jeff (2006c), "An 'Intellectual Tragedy': A Reply to Ken Wilber's 'What We Are, That We See'" (http://www.integralworld.net/meyerhoff5.html).

Meyerhoff, Jeff (2006b), "What's Worthy of Inclusion? A Reply to Mark Edwards" (http://www.integralworld.net/meyerhoff3.html).

Meyerhoff, Jeff (2006a), "Six Criticisms of Wilber's Integral Theory" (http://www.integralworld.net/meyerhoff4.html).

Meyerhoff, Jeff (2006 [2003]), *Bald Ambition: A Critique of Ken Wilber's Theory of Everything* (http://www.integralworld.net/ meyerhoff-ba-toc.html).

Miller, Peter (1995), "Jane Goodall," in *National Geographic,* December.

Minerd, Jeff (2000), *"The Marriage of Sense and Soul* by Ken Wilber," in *Skeptical Inquirer,* Volume 24, No. 1, January/February.

Motoyama, Hiroshi (2000 [1992]), *Karma and Reincarnation: A Key to Spiritual Evolution and Enlightenment* (London: Piatkus).

Murphy, Michael (1998), *The Kingdom of Shivas Irons* (New York: Broadway Books).

Murphy, Michael (1992), *The Future of the Body: Explorations into the Further Evolution of Human Nature* (Los Angeles: Jeremy P. Tarcher, Inc.).

Murphy, Michael, Steven Donovan and Eugene Taylor (1997), *The Physical and Psychological Effects of Meditation: A Review of Contemporary Research with a Comprehensive Bibliography, 1931–1996* (Petaluma, CA: Institute of Noetic Sciences).

Myers, PZ (2007), "Letter to a non-atheist New Atheist" (http://scienceblogs.com/pharyngula/2007/10/letter_to_a_nonatheist_new_ath.php).

Nanda, Meera (2003), "Trading Faith for Spirituality: The Mystifications of Sam Harris" (http://www.butterfliesandwheels.com/articleprint.php?num=161).

Neary, Walt (1985), "Crazy Wisdom Bent Minds, Say Ex-Cultists," in *Lake County Record-Bee,* April 11. (http://web .archive.org/web/20031227113341/lightgate.net/archives/ daism-02/daism-02.mv?module=view&viewid=715&row=228).

Oakes, Len (1997), *Prophetic Charisma: The Psychology of Revolutionary Religious Personalities* (Syracuse, NY: Syracuse University Press).

Odajnyk, V. Walter (1993), *Gathering the Light: A Psychology of Meditation* (Boston, MA: Shambhala Publications, Inc.).

Orr, H. Allen (2005), "Devolution: Why Intelligent Design Isn't," in *The New Yorker,* May 30 (http://www.newyorker.com/fact/content/articles/050530fa_fact).

Papert, Seymour (1993), *Mindstorms: Children, Computers, and Powerful Ideas* (New York: Basic Books).

Park, Robert L. (1997), "Alternative Medicine and the Laws of Physics," in *Skeptical Inquirer,* Volume 21, No. 5, September/ October (http://www.csicop.org/si/9709/park.html).

Parker, Scott (2007), "Winning the Integral Game?" (http://www.integralworld.net/parker.html)

Peat, F. David (1997), *Infinite Potential: The Life and Times of David Bohm* (Reading, MA: Addison-Wesley).

Penny, Bob (1993), *Social Control in Scientology: A Look at the Methods of Entrapment* (http://www-2.cs.cmu.edu/~dst/Library/Shelf/xenu/scs.html).

Phipps, Carter (2007), "The REAL Evolution Debate: Everything you always wanted to know about evolution but the mass media wouldn't tell you," in *What Is Enlightenment?* Issue 35.

Phipps, Carter (2001), "I'm Optimistic: An Interview with Joe Firmage," in *What Is Enlightenment?* Issue 19 (http://www.wie.org/j19/firmage.asp?showRelated=1).

Piaget, Jean (1972), "Intellectual Evolution from Adolescence to Adulthood," in *Human Development,* 15, 1-12.

Piaget, Jean and Bärbel Inhelder (2000 [1969]), *The Psychology of the Child* (New York: Basic Books).

Piaget, Jean (1932), *Moral Judgment of the Child* (New York: Free Press).

Pigliucci, Massimo (2001), "Design Yes, Intelligent No: A Critique of Intelligent Design Theory and Neocreationism," in *Skeptical Inquirer,* Volume 25, No. 4, July/August (http://www.csicop.org/si/2001-09/design.html).

Pinker, Steven (1999 [1997]), *How the Mind Works* (New York: W. W. Norton & Company, Inc.).

Radin, Dean (1997), *The Conscious Universe: The Scientific Truth of Psychic Phenomena* (San Francisco: HarperSanFrancisco).

Radzik, Jody (2005), "The Perils of Pedestalization" (http://www.globalserve.net/~sarlo/Yworship.htm).

Rainforth, Maxwell (2000), "A Rebuttal to 'Voodoo Science'" (http://www.istpp.org/crime_prevention/voodoo_rebuttal.html).

Randi, James (2005), "Swift: Online Newsletter of the JREF," July 15 (http://www.randi.org/jr/071505on.html).

Randi, James (2003), "Swift: Online Newsletter of the JREF," October 24 (http://www.randi.org/jr/102403.html).

Randi, James (2002a), "Swift: Online Newsletter of the JREF," September 6 (http://www.randi.org/jr/090602.html).

Randi, James (2002), "Swift: Online Newsletter of the JREF,"
September 13 (http://www.randi.org/jr/091302.html).

Randi, James (1982), *Flim-Flam! Psychics, ESP, Unicorns and
Other Delusions* (Buffalo, NY: Prometheus Books).

Reynolds, Brad (2004), "Where's Wilber At? The Further Evolution
of Ken Wilber's Integral Vision During the Dawn of the New
Millennium"
(http://wilber.shambhala.com/html/misc/wheres-wilber.pdf).

Robbins, Thomas and Dick Anthony, ed. (1982), *In Gods We Trust:
New Patterns of Religious Pluralism in America* (New Brunswick,
NJ: Transaction Books).

Ross, Rick (2005), "Deepak Chopra"
(http://www.rickross.com/groups/deepakchopra.html).

Ross, Rick (2003), "Is Dick Anthony a Full-Time Professional 'Cult
Apologist'?" in *Cult News,* March 27
(http://www.rickross.com/reference/apologist/apologist44.html).

Rothberg, Donald and Sean Kelly, ed. (1998), *Ken Wilber in
Dialogue: Conversations with Leading Transpersonal Thinkers*
(Wheaton, IL: Quest Books).

Schindler, David, ed. (1986), *Beyond Mechanism: The Universe in
Recent Physics and Catholic Thought* (Lanham, MD: The
University Press of America, Inc.).

Schneider, Dan (2007), "The Dan Schneider Interview 4: Steven
Pinker" (http://www.cosmoetica.com/DSI4.htm).

Schwartz, Gary and Linda Russek (1999), *The Living Energy
Universe: A Fundamental Discovery That Transforms Science &
Medicine* (Charlottesville, VA: Hampton Roads Publishing
Company, Inc.).

Schwartz, Gary with William L. Simon (2002), *The Afterlife
Experiments: Breakthrough Scientific Evidence of Life After Death*
(New York: Atria Books).

Schwartz, Tony (1996), *What Really Matters: Searching for Wisdom in America* (New York: Bantam Books).

Schwendter, Rolf (1991), "Partial cultures, subcultures, pivot persons, plural identities," European Expert Meeting "Overlapping cultures and plural identities" (Vienna, 23-26 May 1991) organised within the framework of the UNESCO World Decade for Cultural Development by the Austrian National Commission for Unesco and "Wiener Denk-Werkstatt" at the Adult Education Academy Brigittenau (http://www.vienna-thinktank.at/ocpi1991/91ocpi_schwendter.htm).

Shambhala (2001), "On Critics, Integral Institute, My Recent Writing, and Other Matters of Little Consequence: A Shambhala Interview with Ken Wilber" (http://wilber.shambhala.com/html/interviews/interview1220_3.cfm/).

Shermer, Michael (2005), "Enigma: The Faustian Bargain of David Irving" (http://www.skeptic.com/eskeptic/05-05-03.html).

Singer, Margaret T. (2003 [1995]), *Cults in Our Midst: The Continuing Fight Against Their Hidden Menace* (San Francisco, CA: John Wiley & Sons, Inc.).

Smith, Andrew P. (2006a), "Holarchic Sense and Holarchic Nonsense" (http://www.integralworld.net/smith23.html).

Smith, Andrew P. (2006), "An IMP Runs Amok: The Promise and the Problems of Wilber's Integral Methodological Pluralism" (http://www.integralworld.net/smith22.html).

Smith, Andrew P. (2004), "Contextualizing Ken: A Review of Jeff Meyerhoff's Bald Ambition" (http://www.integralworld.net/smith20.html).

Smith, Andrew P. (2003), "The Pros and Cons of Pronouns: My View of My View of Edwards' View of Wilber's View of Views" (http://www.integralworld.net/smith19.html).

Smith, Andrew P. (2001a), "Why It Matters: Further Monologues with Ken Wilber" (http://www.integralworld.net/smith14.html).

Smith, Andrew P. (2001), "All Four One and One for All: A (Somewhat Biased) Comparison of the Four Quadrant and One-Scale Models of Holarchy" (http://www.integralworld.net/smith4.html).

Sokal, Alan and Jean Bricmont (1998), *Fashionable Nonsense: Postmodern Intellectuals' Abuse of Science* (New York: St. Martin's Press).

Stenger, Victor J. (2004), "Reality Check: The Evolution of Creationism," in *Skeptical Briefs,* June 2004 (http://www.csicop.org/sb/2004-06/reality-check.html).

Strelley, Kate with Robert D. San Souci (1987), *The Ultimate Game: The Rise and Fall of Bhagwan Shree Rajneesh* (San Francisco, CA: Harper & Row, Publishers).

Suggestibility (2006), "Falling Down the TM® Rabbit Hole: How Transcendental Meditation Really Works, a Critical Opinion" (http://www.suggestibility.org/).

Sullivan, Meg (2005), "Media Bias Is Real, Finds UCLA Political Scientist," in *UCLA Newsroom,* December 14 (http://newsroom.ucla.edu/portal/ucla/Media-Bias-Is-Real-Finds-UCLA-6664.aspx).

Tarlo, Luna (1997), *The Mother of God* (Brooklyn, NY: Plover Press).

Time (1978), "Animals That Kill Their Young," January 9 (http://www.time.com/time/archive/preview/ 0,10987,912086,00.html).

Underwood, Barbara and Betty Underwood (1979), *Hostage to Heaven: Four Years in the Unification Church by an Ex Moonie and the Mother Who Fought to Free Her* (New York: Clarkson N. Potter, Inc.).

Van Biema, David (1996), "Emperor of the Soul: Combining Medical Advice with Indian Metaphysics, Deepak Chopra Has Thrived, Telling Americans of a Place Where Spirit and Body Interact," in *Time,* June 24 (http://www.time.com/time/archive/ preview/0%2C10987%2C1101960624-136108%2C00.html).

Van der Braak, Andre (2003), *Enlightenment Blues: My Years with an American Guru* (Rhinebeck, NY: Monkfish Book Publishing Company).

Van der Horst, Brian (1997), "A Light in the Wilberness" (http://web.archive.org/web/20050308053231/http://www.cs.ucr.edu/~gnick/bvdh/light_in_the_wilberness.htm).

Visser, Frank (2006), "Games Pandits Play: A Reply to Ken Wilber's Raging Rant" (http://www.integralworld.net/visser12.html).

Visser, Frank (2003), *Ken Wilber: Thought As Passion* (Albany, NY: State University of New York Press).

Vomiting Confetti (2005), "Awaken White Morpheus," May 27 (http://vomitingconfetti.blogspot.com/2005/05/awaken-white-morpheus.html).

Wade, Jenny (1996), *Changes of Mind* (Albany, NY: State University of New York Press).

Walsh, Roger and Frances Vaughan, ed. (1993), *Paths Beyond Ego: The Transpersonal Vision* (Los Angeles: Jeremy P. Tarcher, Inc.).

Walsh, Roger and Frances Vaughan, ed. (1988), *A Gift of Healing: Selections from A Course in Miracles* (Los Angeles: Jeremy P. Tarcher, Inc.).

Weber, Renee (1986), *Dialogues with Scientists and Sages: The Search for Unity* (New York: Routledge and Kegan Paul).

WHAT Enlightenment??! (2005), "WHAT enlightenment??! An Uncensored Look at Self-Styled 'Guru' Andrew Cohen" (http://whatenlightenment.blogspot.com).

White, John (1997b), "Foreword to the Twentieth-Anniversary Edition (1997)," in Ken Wilber (1999c), *Collected Works,* Volume 1 (Boston, MA: Shambhala).

White, John (1997), "The Experience of God-Realization," in *Noumenon: A Newsletter for the Nondual Perspective* (http://www.noumenon.co.za/html/summer_1997.html).

Wikipedia (2006c), "Addiction"
(http://en.wikipedia.org/wiki/Addiction).

Wikipedia (2006b), "Narcissism (Psychology)"
(http://en.wikipedia.org/wiki/Narcissism_%28psychology%29).

Wikipedia (2006a), "Ressentiment"
(http://en.wikipedia.org/wiki/Ressentiment).

Wikipedia (2006), "Amnesty International"
(http://en.wikipedia.org/wiki/Amnesty_International).

Wilber, Ken (2007a), "Ken explains how he can synthesize so much
information...." (http://kenwilber.meetup.com/boards/view/
viewthread?thread=2824036).

Wilber, Ken (2007), "Re: Some Criticisms of My Understanding of
Evolution" (http://www.kenwilber.com/blog/show/390).

Wilber, Ken (2006e), *Integral Spirituality: A Startling New Role for
Religion in the Modern and Postmodern World* (Boston, MA:
Integral Books).

Wilber, Ken (2006d), "Take the Visser Site as Alternatives to KW,
But Never as the Views of KW"
(http://www.kenwilber.com/blog/show/86).

Wilber, Ken (2006c), "What Would Wyatt Do? Follow-Up #3"
(http://www.kenwilber.com/blog/show/83).

Wilber, Ken (2006b), "On the Nature of Shadow Projections in
Forums. Follow-Up #2"
(http://www.kenwilber.com/blog/show/50).

Wilber, Ken (2006a), "What We Are, That We See. Part II: What is
the Real Meaning of This?"
(http://www.kenwilber.com/blog/show/48).

Wilber, Ken (2006), "What We Are, That We See. Part I: Response
to Some Recent Criticism in a Wild West Fashion"
(http://www.kenwilber.com/blog/show/46).

Wilber, Ken (2005a), "The Taboo of (Inter)Subjectivity. Part 2. Why Does Dirt Get Up and Start Writing Poetry?" on *Integral Naked,* June 20 (http://in.integralinstitute.org/contributor.aspx?id=79).

Wilber, Ken (2005), "Q-Munity Reviews" (http://web.archive.org/web/20061019003329/http://www.clarus.co m/q_qmunity_reviews.shtml).

Wilber, Ken (2004a), "Ken Stops His Brain Waves!" (http://www.integralnaked.org/news/index.aspx).

Wilber, Ken (2004), "A Suggestion for Reading the Criticisms of My Work" (http://www.integralworld.net/wilber_wokw.html).

Wilber, Ken (2003d), "The War in Iraq" (http://wilber.shambhala.com/html/misc/iraq.cfm).

Wilber, Ken (2003c), *Kosmic Consciousness* (Boulder, CO: Sounds True).

Wilber, Ken (2003b), "Excerpt C: The Ways We Are in This Together: Intersubjectivity and Interobjectivity in the Holonic Kosmos" (http://wilber.shambhala.com/html/books/kosmos/ excerptC/intro-1.cfm).

Wilber, Ken (2003a), "On the Nature of a Post-Metaphysical Spirituality: Response to Habermas and Weis" (http://wilber.shambhala.com/html/misc/habermas/partII.cfm).

Wilber, Ken (2003), "Excerpt G: Toward a Comprehensive Theory of Subtle Energies" (http://wilber.shambhala.com/html/books/ kosmos/excerptG/part1.cfm).

Wilber, Ken (2002), "RNase Enzyme Deficiency Disease: Wilber's Statement About His Health" (http://www.integralworld.net/redd.html).

Wilber, Ken (2001d), *Speaking of Everything* (Menlo Park, CA: Enlightenment.Com).

Wilber, Ken (2001c), "Do Critics Misrepresent My Position? A Test Case from a Recent Academic Journal" (http://wilber.shambhala.com/html/misc/critics_01.cfm).

Wilber, Ken (2001b), *A Theory of Everything: An Integral Vision for Business, Politics, Science and Spirituality* (Boston, MA: Shambhala).

Wilber, Ken (2001a [1979]), *No Boundary: Eastern and Western Approaches to Personal Growth* (Boston, MA: Shambhala).

Wilber, Ken (2001), *Boomeritis: A Novel That Will Set You Free!* (Boston, MA: Shambhala).

Wilber, Ken (2000f), "Introduction to Volume 7 of the *Collected Works*" (http://wilber.shambhala.com/html/books/cowokev7_intro.cfm#fnB7).

Wilber, Ken (2000e), "Waves, Streams, States, and Self—A Summary of My Psychological Model (Or, Outline of an Integral Psychology)" (http://wilber.shambhala.com/html/books/psych_model/psych_model1.cfm).

Wilber, Ken (2000d), "Announcing the Formation of Integral Institute" (http://wilber.shambhala.com/html/books/formation_int_inst.cfm).

Wilber, Ken (2000c [1996]), *A Brief History of Everything* (Boston, MA: Shambhala).

Wilber, Ken (2000b), *Integral Psychology: Consciousness, Spirit, Psychology, Therapy* (Boston, MA: Shambhala).

Wilber, Ken (2000a), *One Taste: The Journals of Ken Wilber* (Boston, MA: Shambhala).

Wilber, Ken (2000), *Sex, Ecology, Spirituality,* second edition (Boston, MA: Shambhala).

Wilber, Ken (1999c), *Collected Works,* Volume 1 (Boston, MA: Shambhala).

Wilber, Ken (1999b), "Introduction to the Fourth Volume 4 [*sic*] of the *Collected Works*" (http://wilber.shambhala.com/html/books/cowokev4_intro.cfm/xid%2C3419/yid%2C4006550).

Wilber, Ken (1999a [1998]), *The Marriage of Sense and Soul: Integrating Science and Religion* (New York: Broadway Books).

Wilber, Ken (1999), "Ken Wilber's Response to John Heron" (http://www.integralworld.net/heron.html).

Wilber, Ken (1998b), "An Update on the Case of Adi Da" (http://wilber.shambhala.com/html/misc/adida_update.cfm).

Wilber, Ken (1998a), "Letter to the Adi Da Community" (http://www.beezone.com/Wilber/ken_wilbers_letter.html).

Wilber, Ken (1998), *The Eye of Spirit: An Integral Vision for a World Gone Slightly Mad* (Boston, MA: Shambhala).

Wilber, Ken (1996a), "The Case of Adi Da" (http://wilber.shambhala.com/html/misc/adida.cfm).

Wilber, Ken (1996), *A Brief History of Everything* (Boston, MA: Shambhala).

Wilber, Ken (1995), *Sex, Ecology, and Spirituality* (Boston, MA: Shambhala).

Wilber, Ken (1991), *Grace and Grit: Spirituality & Healing in the Life & Death of Treya Killam Wilber* (Boulder, CO: Shambhala).

Wilber, Ken (1983b), *A Sociable God: Toward a New Understanding of Religion* (Boulder, CO: Shambhala).

Wilber, Ken (1983a), *Up from Eden* (Boulder, CO: Shambhala).

Wilber, Ken (1983), *Eye to Eye* (Boulder, CO: Shambhala).

Wilber, Ken (1982), *The Holographic Paradigm and Other Paradoxes* (Boulder, CO: Shambhala).

Wilber, Ken (1980), *The Atman Project: A Transpersonal View of Human Development* (Boulder, CO: Shambhala).

Wilber, Ken (1977), *The Spectrum of Consciousness* (Wheaton, IL: The Theosophical Publishing House).

Zablocki, Benjamin (2001), "Methodological Fallacies in Anthony's Critique of Exit Cost Analysis" (http://www.rci.rutgers.edu/~zablocki/Anthony.htm).

Zimbardo, Philip G. (2004b), "A Situationist Perspective on the Psychology of Evil: Understanding How Good People are Transformed into Perpetrators," in A. G. Miller, ed., *The Social Psychology of Good and Evil* (New York: Guilford Press; chapter text available online at http://www.prisonexp.org/pdf/evil.pdf).

Zimbardo, Philip G. (2004), "Stanford Prison Experiment Slide Show" (http://www.prisonexp.org).

# INDEX

Acupuncture, 137
Alexander, Charles
    experimental methodology of, 36-43, 47
Amnesty International, 65-8
Anthony, Dick, 106-8, 122
Archetypes, 22-3
Astral travel, 34, 47, 137, 145
Astrology, 51, 64
Atheism, 75, 81, 145, 147
Atman, 19, 24, 121
Aurobindo, 1, 50-1

Bauwens, Michel, 82, 93, 99-100, 105
Beck, Don, 28, 85, 100
Behe, Michael, 8-11, 13-4
Bell, J. S., 165, 169
Bennis, Warren, 144
Bentov, Itzhak, 33, 167
Bohm, David, 18-9, 73, 75, 93, 96, 131-2, 149-176
    Green's function, 153-4
    holomovement of, 151, 153, 159, 169; see also Holograms
    implicate/explicate order of, 149-63, 166-70
    quantum potential of, 151, 156-7, 161
    unitary transformation, 153
Bonder, Saniel, 116, 145
Boomeritis, 28-31, 57, 100
Brainwashing, 85, 107-9; see also Cults
Brainwaves, 57
Branden, Nathaniel, 35, 144
Brennan, Barbara Ann, 50, 52, 58

Cannibalism, animal, viii, 19, 21, 146
Chakras, 10, 52, 55-6
Chamberlain, Jim, 18-9, 101-2
Chopra, Deepak, 2, 56, 60, 143, 145-6
Clinton, Bill, 63, 143

Cohen, Andrew, 107, 112-4, 127-9, 145
Community verification, 33-4, 44-5, 76, 82-3, 115, 138, 162; see also Meditation, and group bias
Copenhagen interpretation, 154, 161-2, 166; see also Bohm, David
Cowan, Christopher, 28-9, 76; see also Spiral Dynamics
Crittenden, Jack, 1, 8, 23
Cults, viii, 44, 84-5, 105, 109, 115, 117-8
    and Iraq war, 68-9
    Wilber's community as, 74, 76, 85-6, 88, 96, 100, 102-3, 105-6, 108-10, 129, 148

Da, Adi, 33, 102, 107, 112-29, 145
    manifested corona of, 33-4, 121, 145
Dallman, Matthew, 82, 93, 104, 106, 110
Darwin, Charles, 6-9, 11-4, 24, 135, 172
Davis, Stuart, 97-8, 145
Dawkins, Richard, 6, 8-9, 13
De Broglie, Louis, 156, 165
De Quincey, Christian, 71-3, 145, 174
Design, Intelligent; see Wilber, Ken, and neo-Darwinian evolution
Dossey, Larry, 12, 56-7, 143, 145

Einstein, Albert, 1, 10, 61-2, 73, 82, 94, 131-2, 135, 139-40, 161-2, 165, 172-3
Elephants, 16-7
Energy, subtle, 49-52, 55-6
    sensed by Wilber, 50
Epicycles, 166-70, 172-3
Eros, 8, 13-7, 48
Evolution; see Wilber, Ken, and neo-Darwinian evolution

Feynman, Richard, 33, 133, 162, 165, 169
Firmage, Joe, 100, 144

Gardner, Howard, 26-8, 77
Gardner, Martin, 32, 57, 161
Goethean, 74-6
Goodall, Jane, 20
Gottfredson, Linda, 27
Great Chain of Being, 15, 150, 155, 157, 166
Greenpeace, 67-8

Hargens, Sean, 71-2
Harris, Sam, 145-7
Hassan, Steve, 117, 129
Heron, John, 45, 174
Holograms, 158-60
Homeopathy, 137
Houston, Jean, 63
Hyman, Ray, 58, 143

Immune system, 13-4, 51
Integral
    Institute (I-I), 2, 12, 23, 28, 44, 60, 67, 71-2, 89, 95-6, 99-102, 104-6, 109, 143-4, 147
    University (IU), 2, 82, 96
    World, 18, 100

Jonestown, 87, 116, 123, 125
Jung, Carl, 22-3, 126

Kauffman, Stuart, 16
Koestler, Arthur, 3
Krippner, Stanley, 57
Kundalini, 50
Kurzweil, Ray, 16

Lane, David, 5, 7-8, 11, 54, 99, 102, 120, 122, 126, 129, 174, 176
Lerner, Michael, 63, 143
Loevinger, Jane, 15, 36-44, 84, 140
Lorenz, Konrad, 21

Mack, John E., 98, 144
Maharishi, 39, 41, 57, 107, 143
    Effect, viii, 57

Mandelbrot, Benoit, 73, 82
Meditation, 3, 5, 32-3, 89, 107, 124
    and group bias, 32-4
    and purported stage-growth, 36-8, 40-3, 44, 46-8, 137; see also Alexander, Charles
    dangers of, viii, 37-8, 45-6, 138
Memes, viii, 29-30, 67, 87, 147
Meyerhoff, Jeff, 17, 26, 44, 77-82, 84, 90, 93-5, 97, 101, 109-10, 174
Motoyama, Hiroshi, 55-6
Murphy, Michael, 2, 45-6, 56, 144

Nanda, Meera, 146
Neocreationism; see Wilber, Ken, and neo-Darwinian evolution
Nietzsche, 1, 93, 137

Odajnyk, V. Walter , 22-3

Papert, Seymour, 25-6
Pauli, Wolfgang, 45, 80
Piaget, Jean, 24-6, 43-4, 53, 91
Pinker, Steven, 15-7, 28
Planck, Max, 44-5
Plato, 79
Prana, 55, 155
Prayer, effects of, viii, 46-8, 56, 64-5, 143
Pre-rationality, 23, 51-2, 54-5, 82, 84, 127, 146-7
Pythagorean Theorem, 61-2

Radin, Dean, 58-9, 145
Rajneesh, 106, 121, 124-5
Rand, Ayn, 44, 144
Randi, James, 12, 57-9, 64, 145
    Paranormal Challenge of, 58
Remote-viewing, 34, 145
Resentiment, 93
ReVision magazine, 2, 8, 156
Reynolds, Brad, 2, 121
Richards, Bob, 60, 145
Robbins, Tony, 145
Ross, Rick, 74

Sai Baba, 107, 124
Schlitz, Marilyn, 57, 145

Schwartz, Gary, 12, 57, 143
Sheldrake, Rupert, 12, 56
*Skeptical Inquirer,* 32, 57
Skeptical Investigations, 12, 59
Smith
    Andrew, 3, 78, 90, 98
    Huston, 91, 102
Spiral Dynamics®, 28-9, 76, 85; *see
    also* Wilber, Ken, on second tier
*Spiritual Choices,* 105-7, 130
*Stripping the Gurus,* vii, 74-5, 85, 106
Superstring theory, 159, 163-4

Tarlo, Luna, 113
Thompson, Keith, 72-3, 145, 173
Thurman, Robert, 144-5
Transcendental Meditation® (TM®),
    37, 41, 46-7, 106
Trungpa, Chögyam, 107, 122, 126-7

Van der Braak, Andre, 113-4
Van der Horst, Brian, 3, 5, 145
Velikovsky, Immanual, 94, 133, 135
Visser, Frank, 18, 99, 101

Wade, Jenny, 149
Walsh, Roger, 90, 144
White, John, 139-40
Whitehead, Alfred North, 1, 14, 79
Wikipedia, 66, 74-6, 87, 103, 105
Wilber, Ken
    and criticism, 91-3, 98
    and cults; *see* Cults, Wilber's
        community as
    and David Bohm; *see* Bohm,
        David
    and Jung; *see* Jung, Carl
    and evolution, 5-19, 24-5, 36, 48,
        79, 111, 137, 147, 172
    and nonexclusion, 79
    and paranormal winds, 53-7,
        104
    and Piaget; *see* Piaget, Jean
    and Q-Link, 52, 59-60, 145
    and REDD, 51
    and responsibility, 52

and subtle energies; *see* Energy,
    subtle
as "Einstein," 1, 10, 131-2, 139-
    40, 173
endorsements of
    psi/parapsychology, 49-60
enlightenment of, 1, 3-4; *see also*
    One Taste realization of
false humility of, 129-30
four-quadrants of (AQAL), 2-3,
    8, 38, 44, 60, 78-9, 83, 92,
    142
hallucinations of, 79
mathematics of, 61-2
narcissism of, 54, 100, 102-3,
    105, 110, 123, 140
on animal cannibalism; *see*
    Cannibalism, animal
on "crazy wisdom," 112-20, 124-
    6
on "liberal media," 63-4
on ozone, 67
on prayer; *see* Prayer, effects of
on postmodernism, 11, 30, 141,
    174
on second tier, 28-30, 48, 84, 87,
    90-1, 93, 96-9, 103, 110,
    137, 147
on shadow-projection, 95-6, 99,
    103
on Spiral Dynamics; *see* Spiral
    Dynamics
on stage-growth; *see* Meditation
on third tier, 96
on war in Iraq, 65-7
One Taste realization of, 4, 51,
    67, 114, 169
orienting generalizations of, 80
phases of work, 23, 169-70
polemics of, 174-5
twenty tenets of, 78
"Wilber police," 72-3, 145

Zen, 4, 46-7, 107, 112-4, 145
Zimbardo, Philip, 69, 84

# ABOUT
# THE AUTHOR

Geoffrey D. Falk (www.geoffreyfalk.com) is author of *The Science of the Soul: On Consciousness and the Structure of Reality, Hip Like Me: Years in the Life of a "Person of Hair,"* and *Stripping the Gurus: Sex, Violence, Abuse and Enlightenment.* He studied electrical engineering and physics at the University of Manitoba. Following that, he kicked ass as a best-in-class computer programmer. He currently divides his time between writing, software development (www.crmfrontiers.com), and music composition (www.my space.com/geoffreyfalk).

CPSIA information can be obtained at www.ICGtesting.com
Printed in the USA
LVOW101305100413

328490LV00001B/3/P